AF575978

DOG HOUSES

Mark Ruwedel

AUGUST EDITIONS

#1 Wonder Valley, CA, 2003

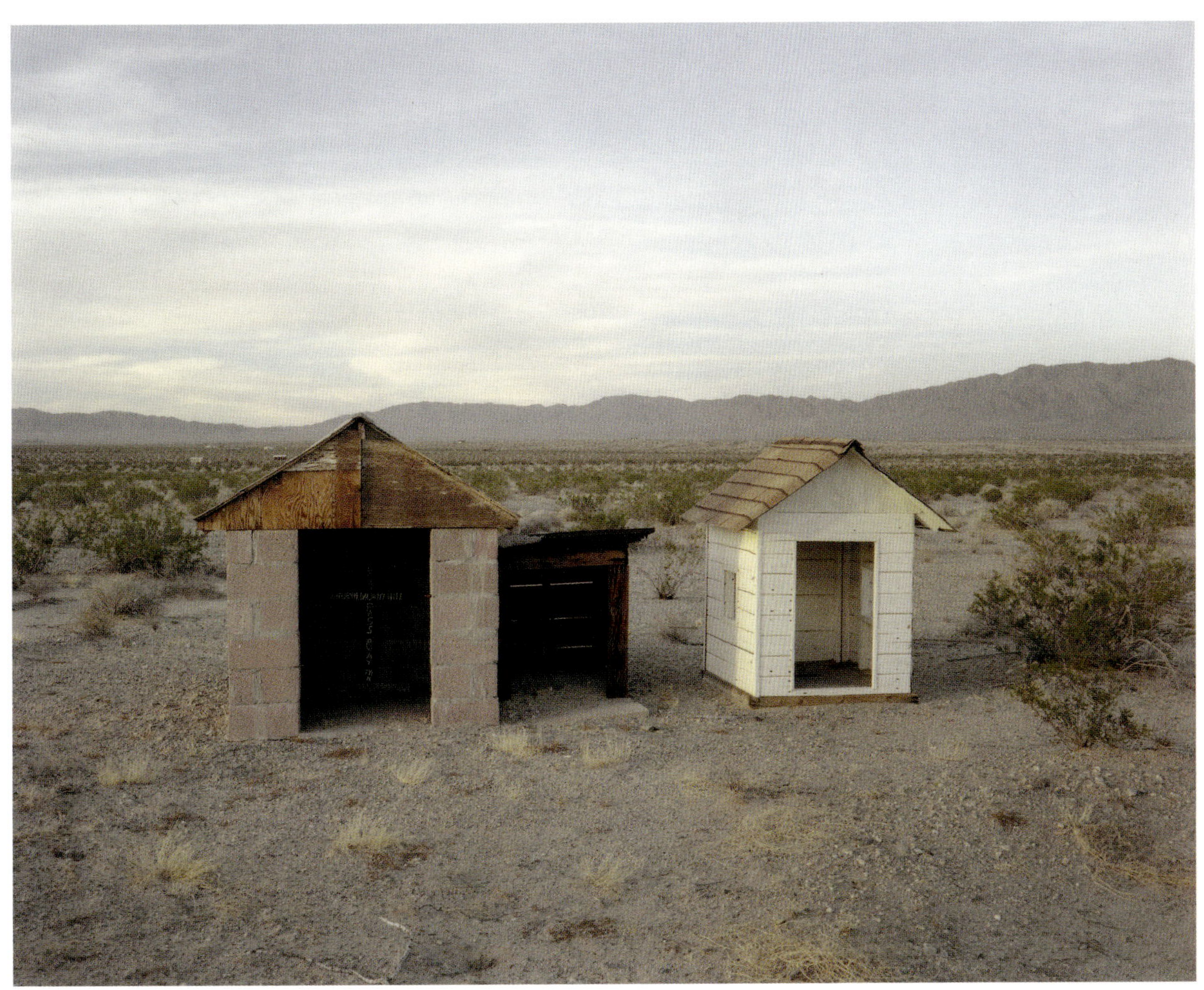

#2 Hinkley, CA, 2005

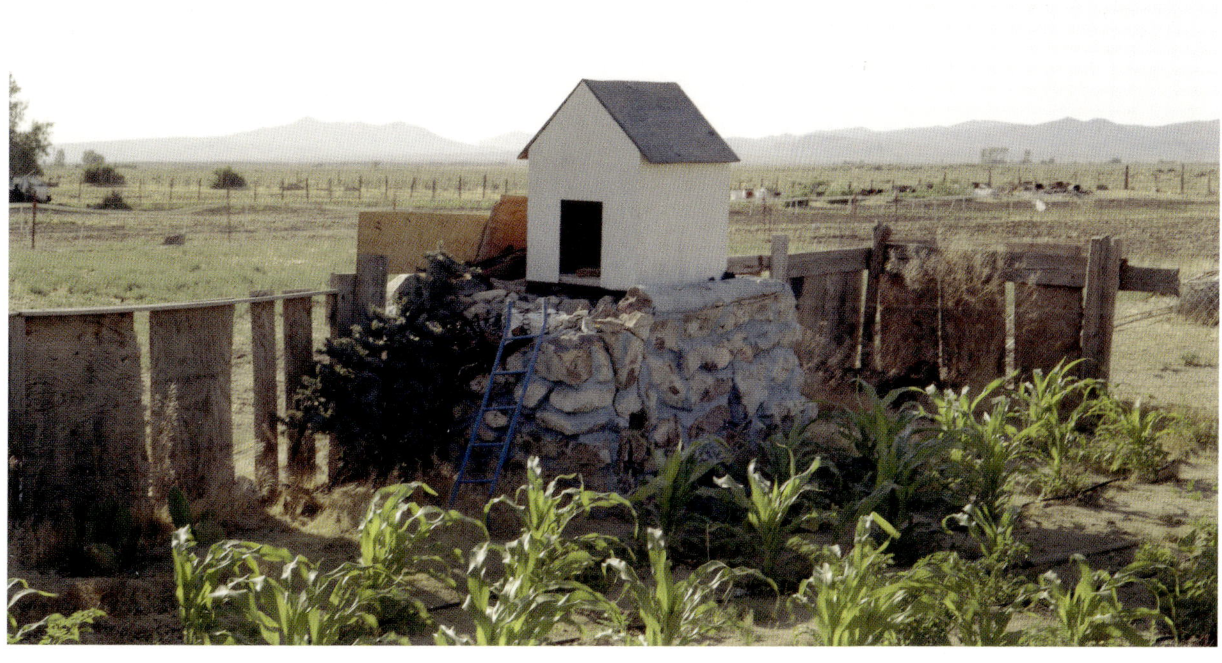

#4 Palm Springs, CA, 2005

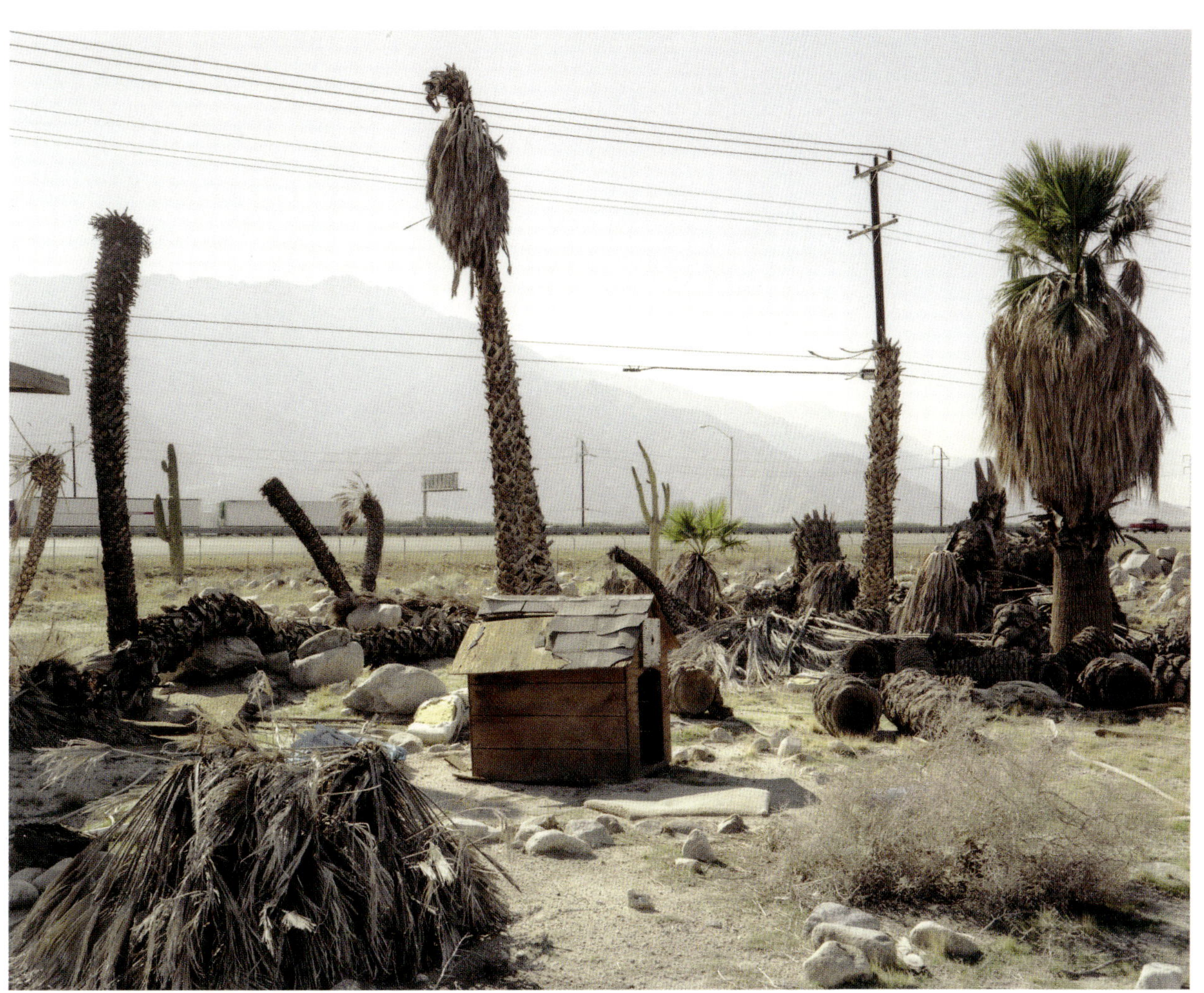

#5 Slab City, CA, 2005

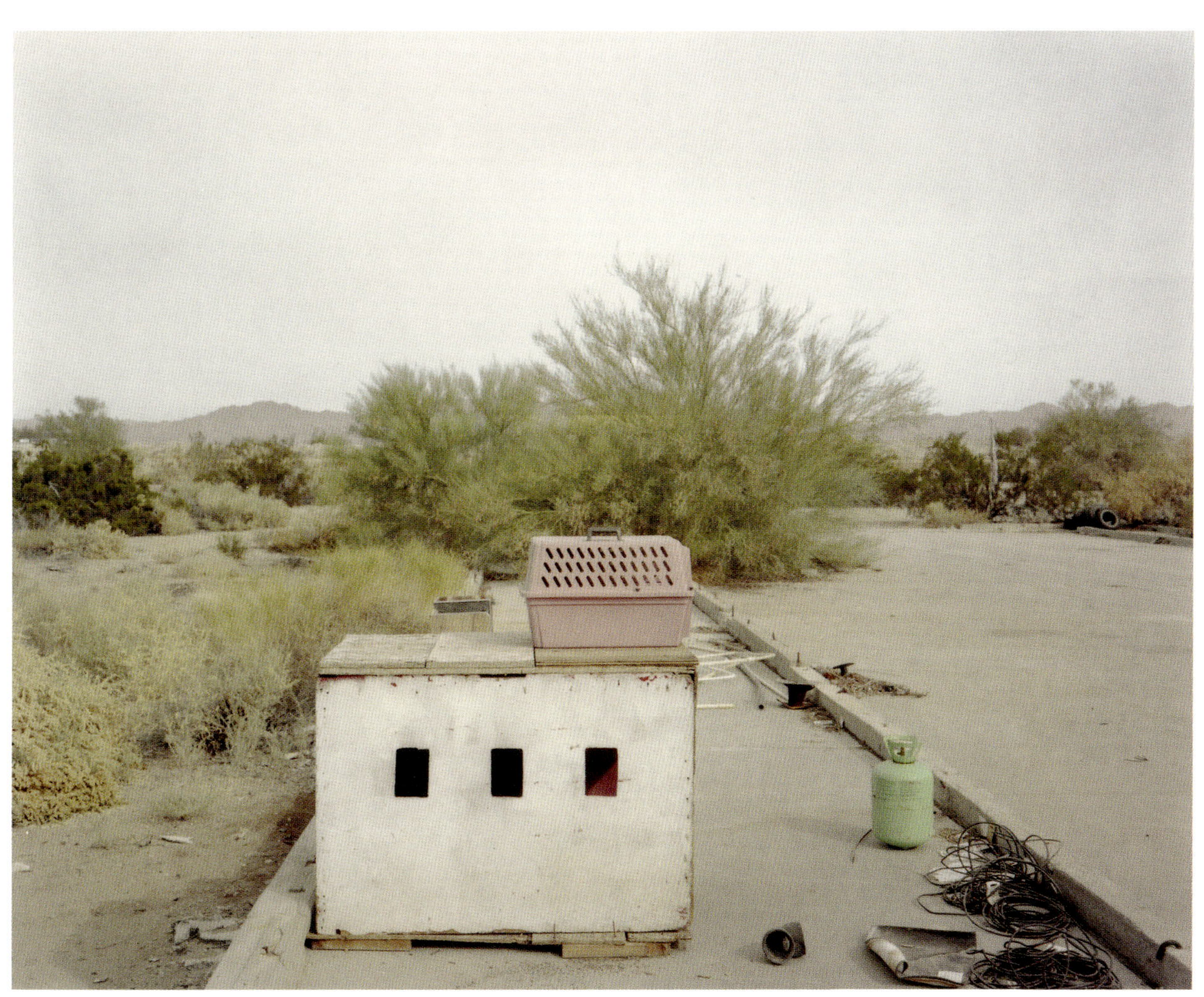

#6 Leeland, NV, 2006

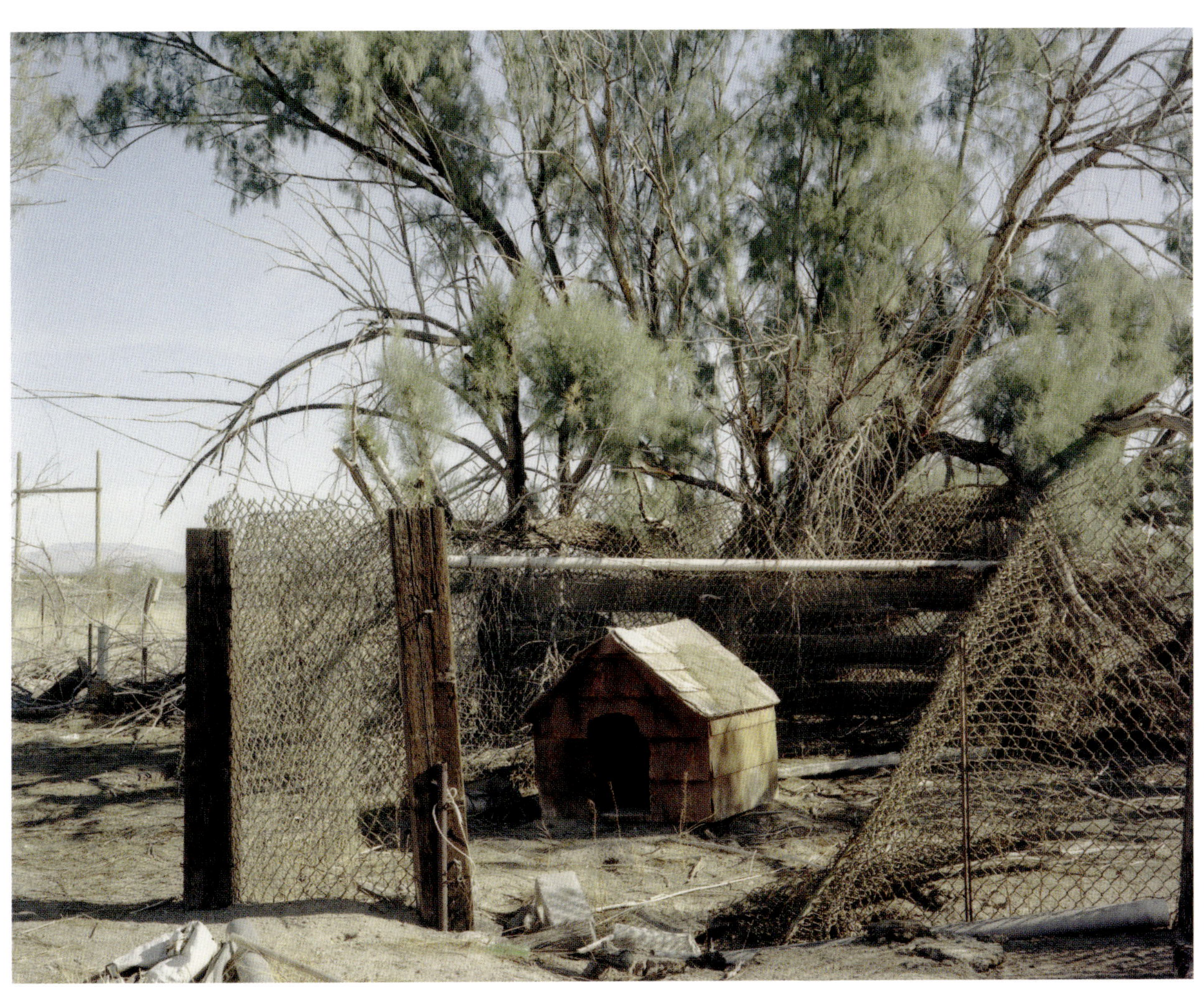

#7 Hinkley, CA, 2006

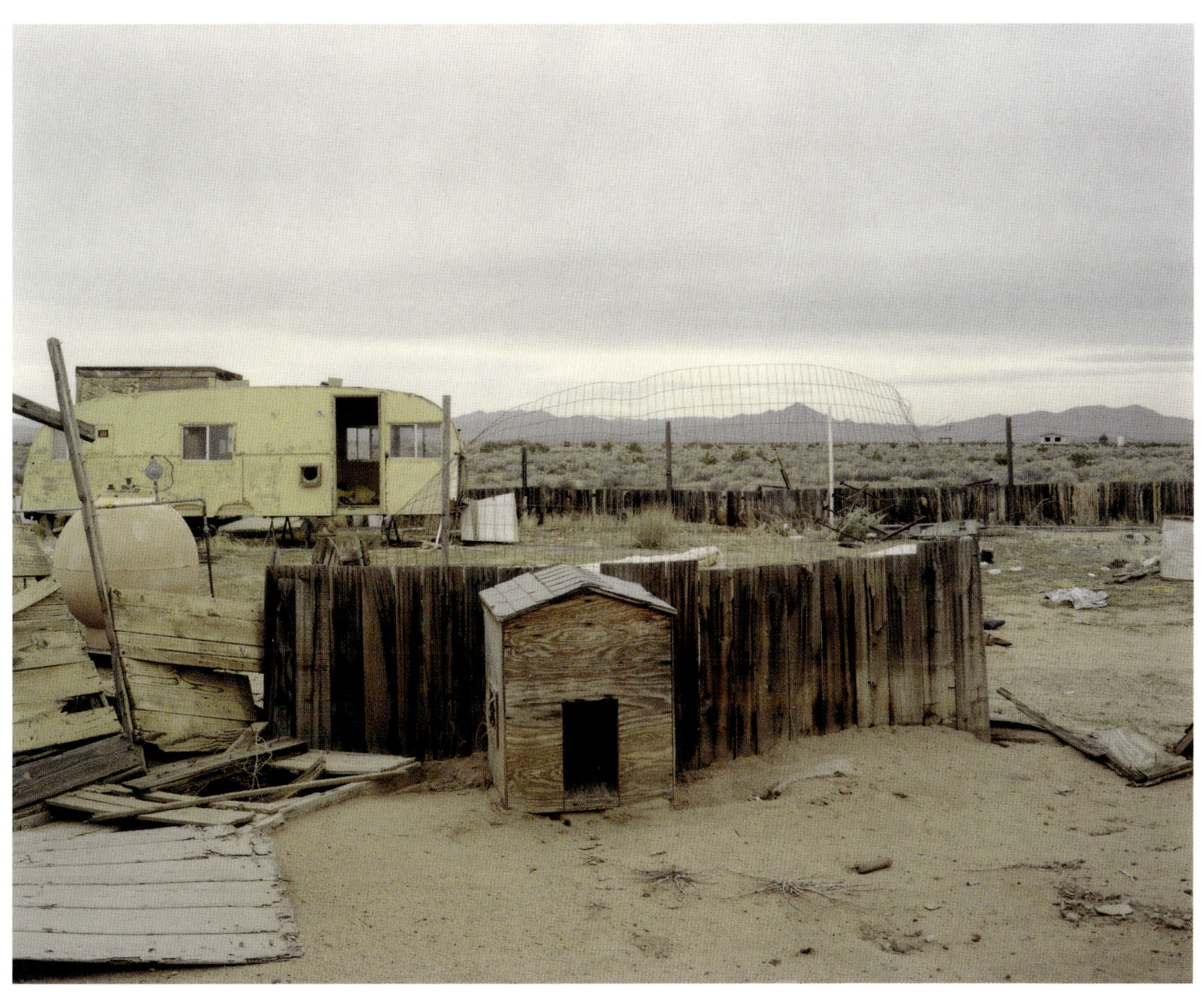

#8 Hinkley, CA, 2006

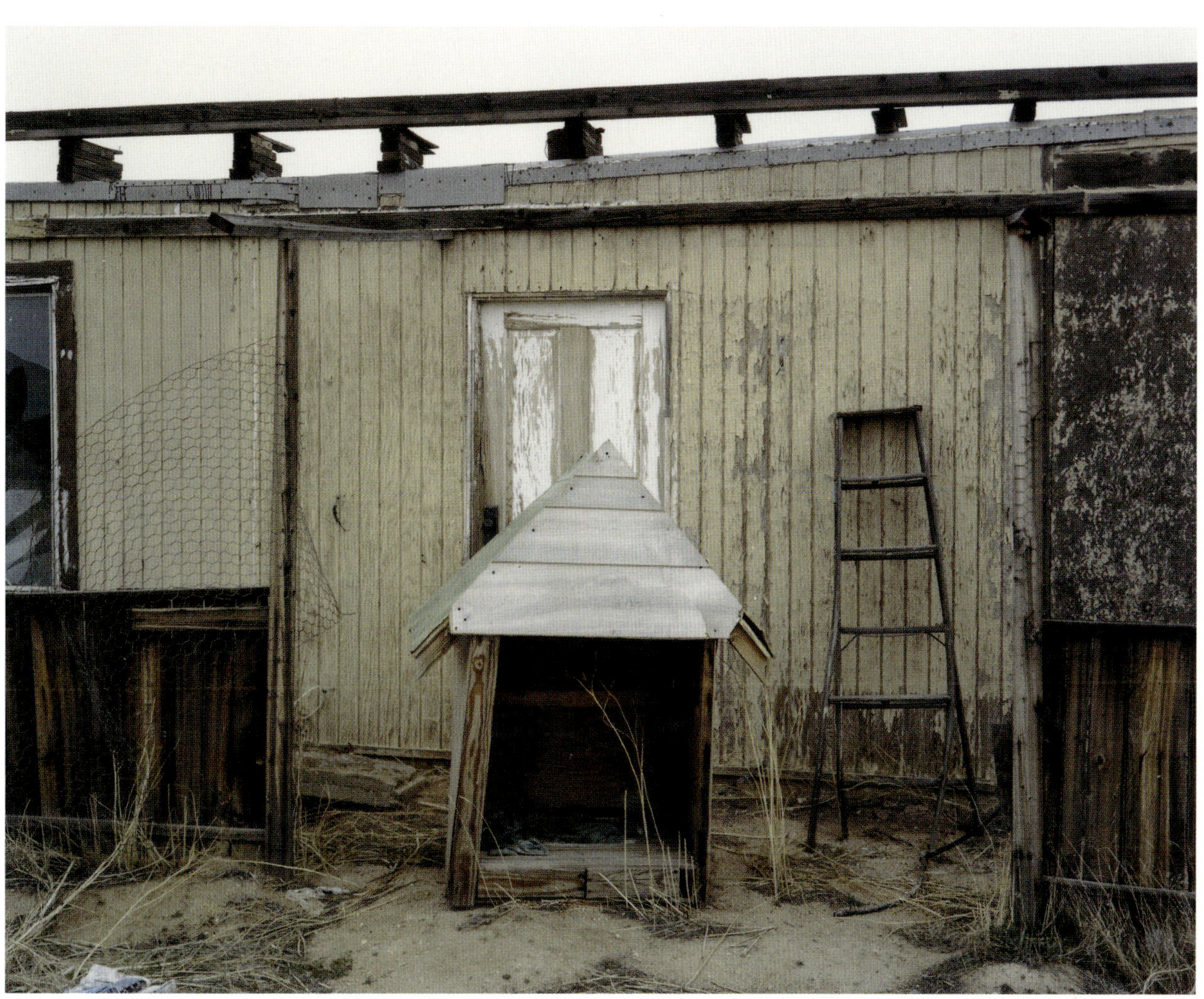

#9 Lucerne Valley, CA, 2006

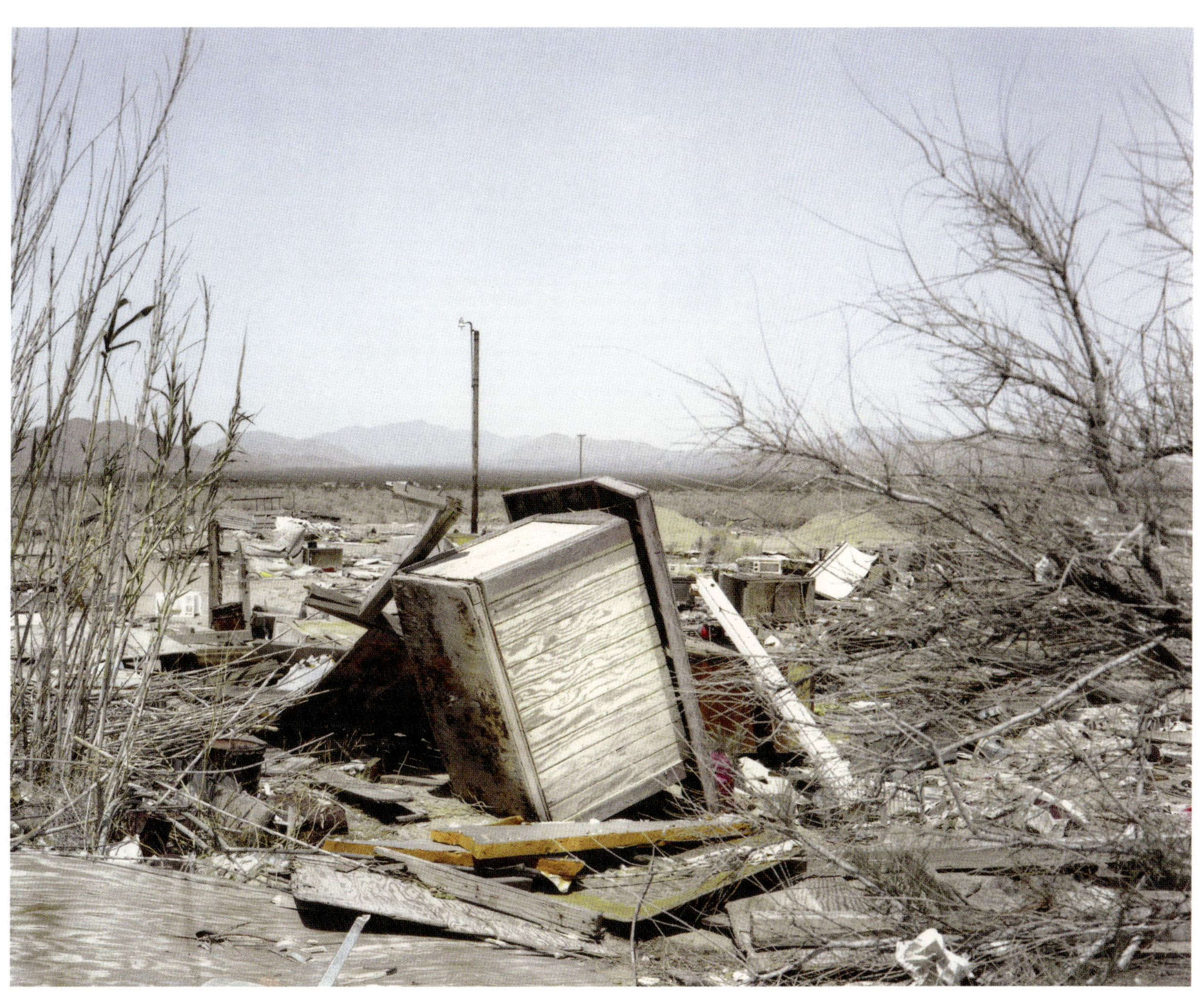

#10 Lucerne Valley, CA, 2006

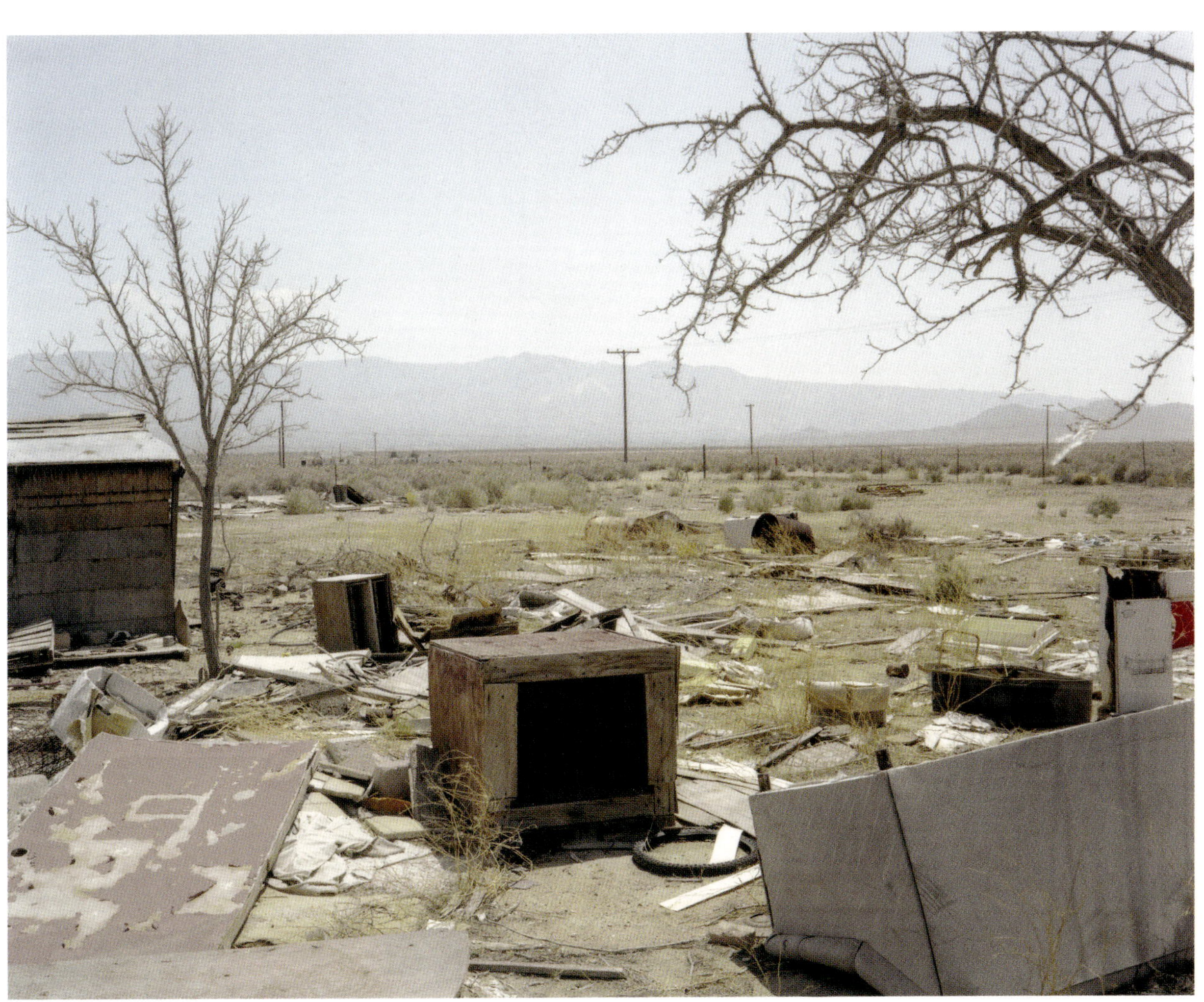

#13 Hinkley, CA, 2006

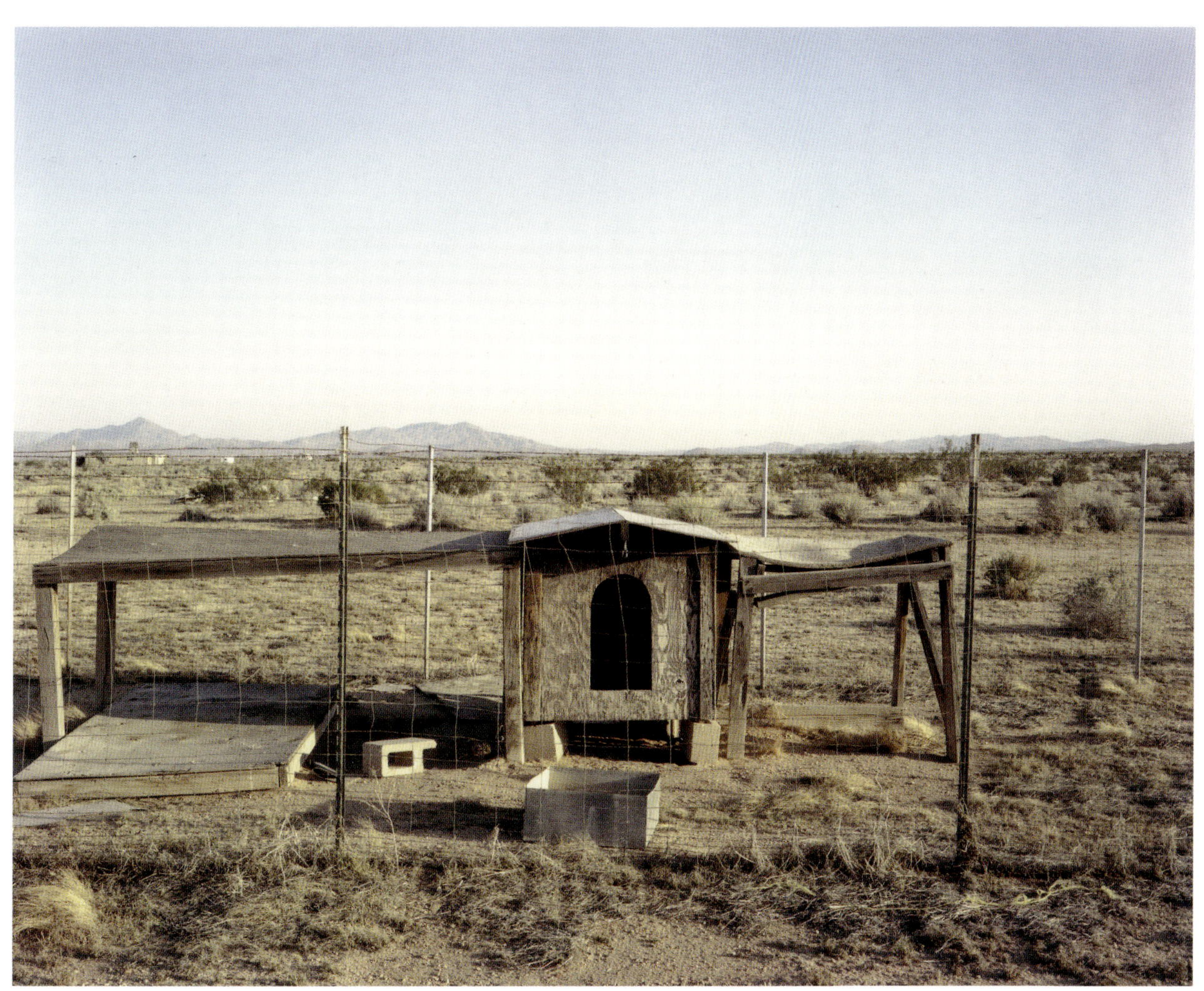

#15 Lucerne Valley, CA, 2007

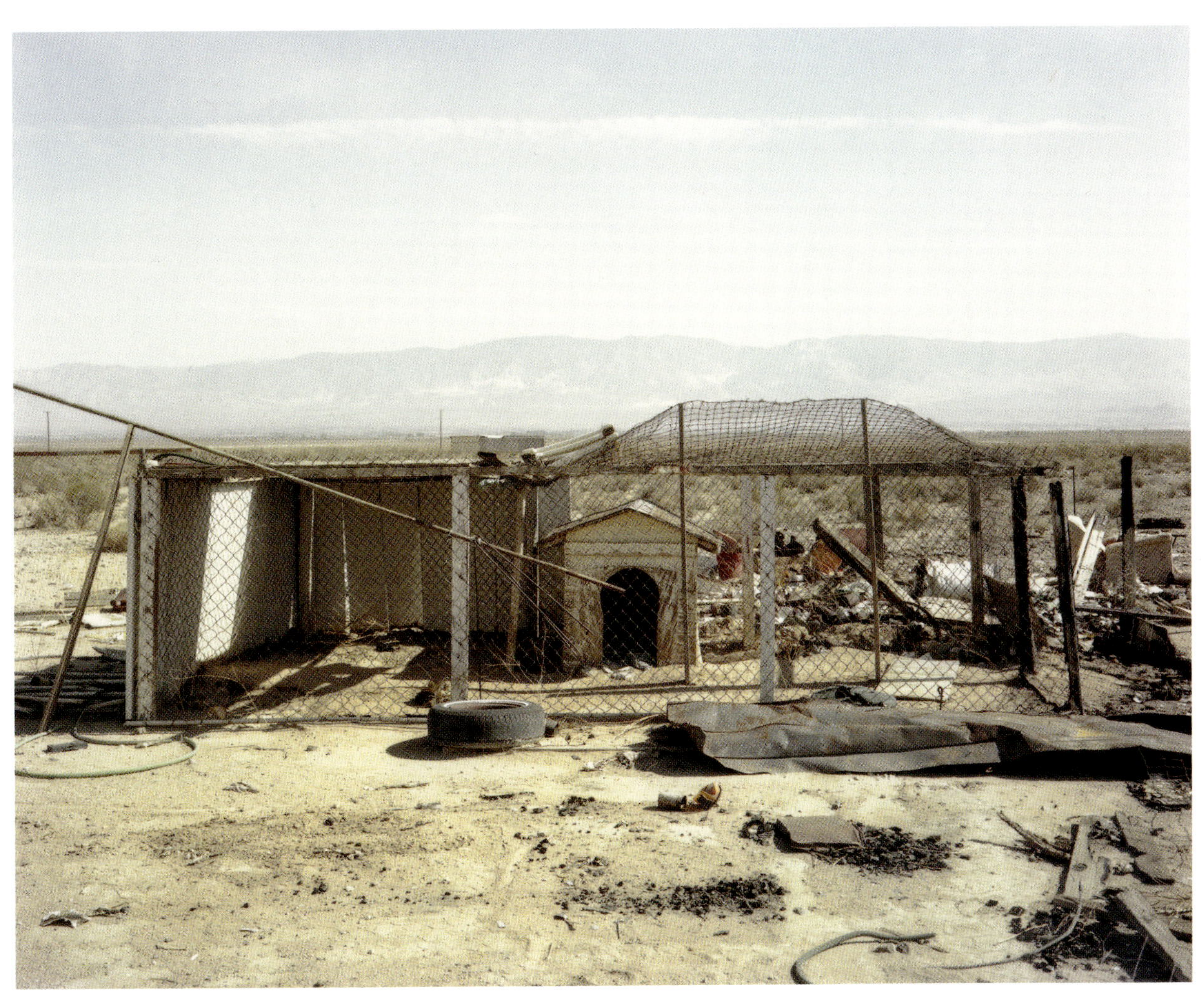

#16 Lucerne Valley, CA, 2007

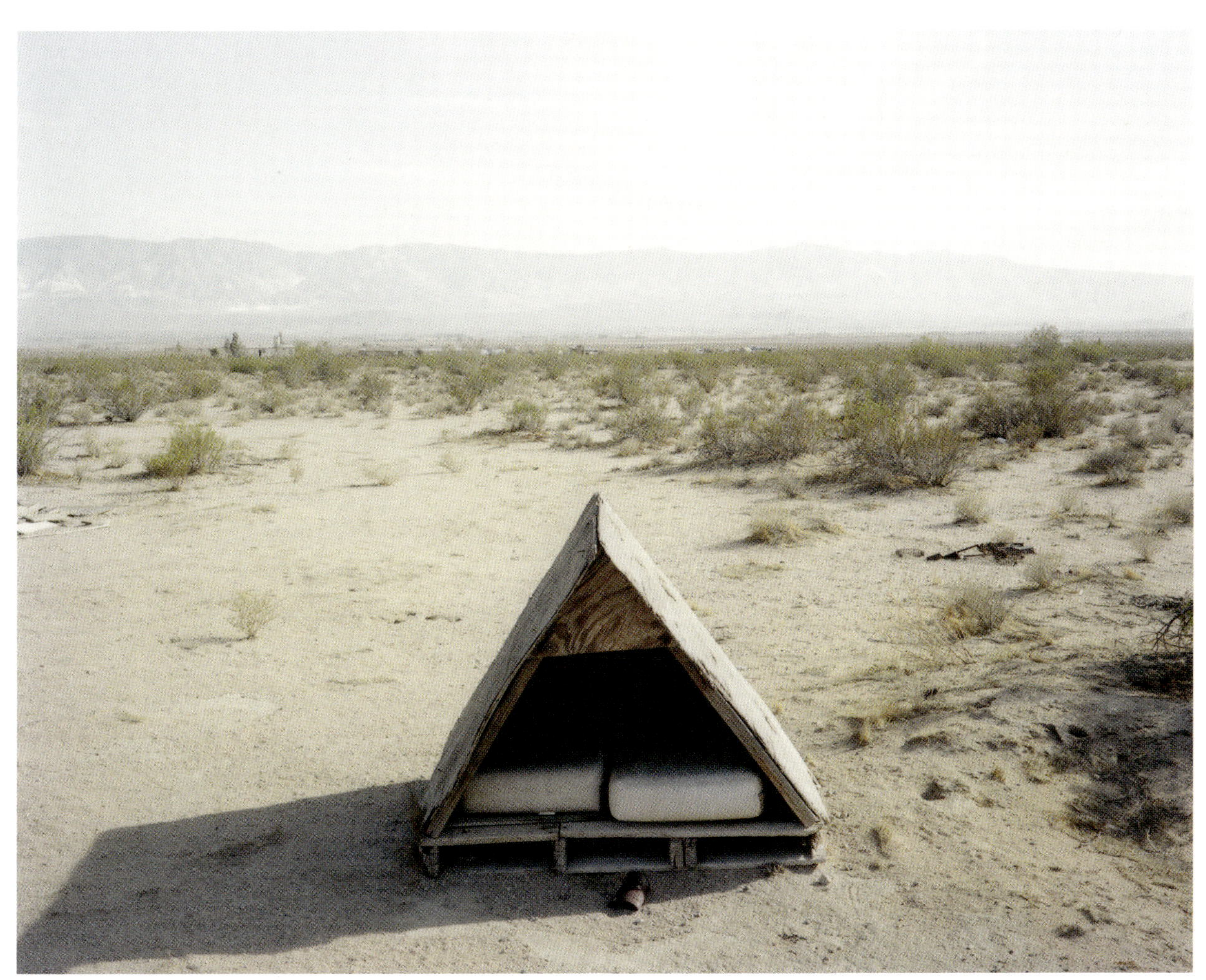

#17 Lucerne Valley, CA, 2007

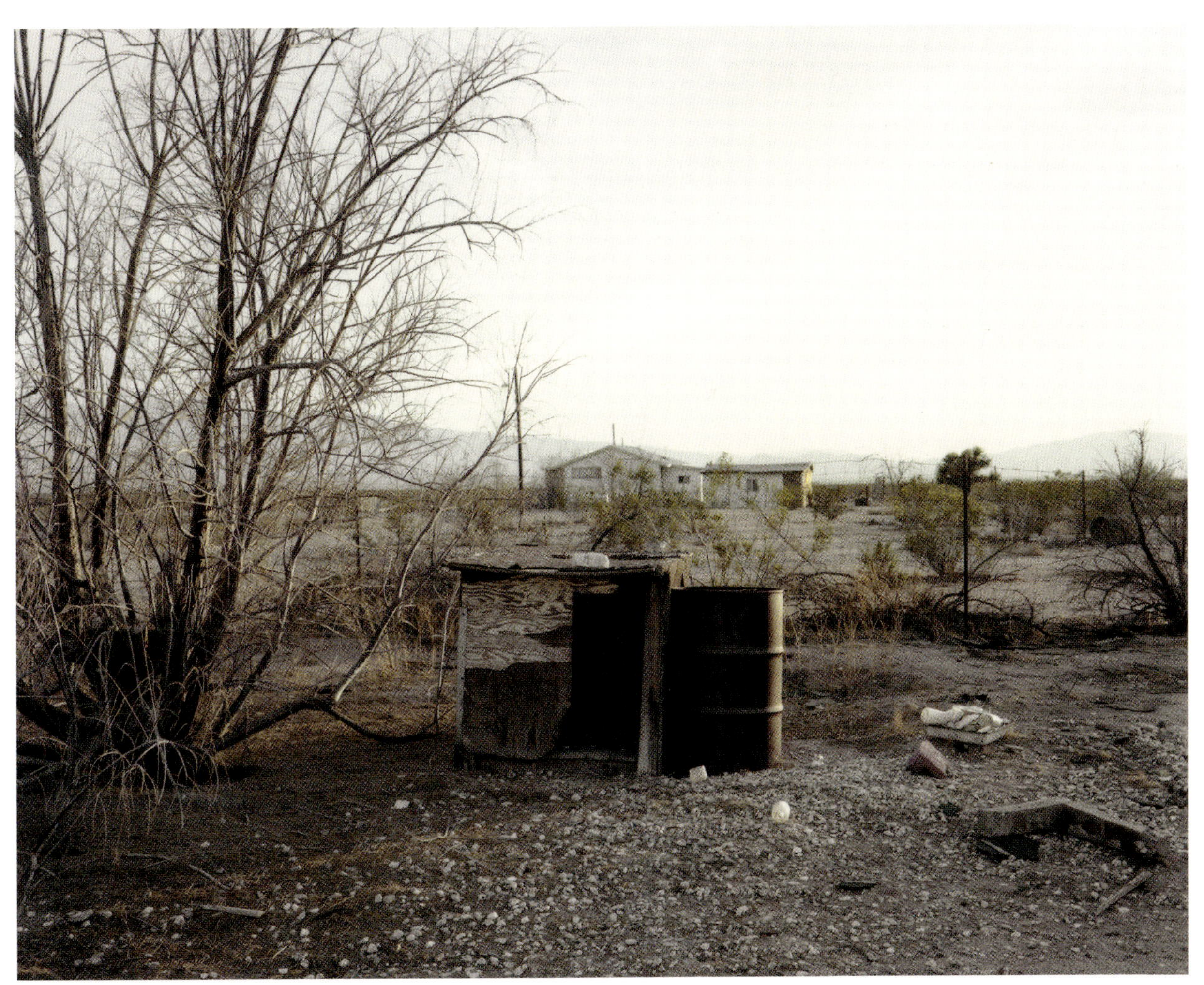

#18 Seeley, CA, 2007

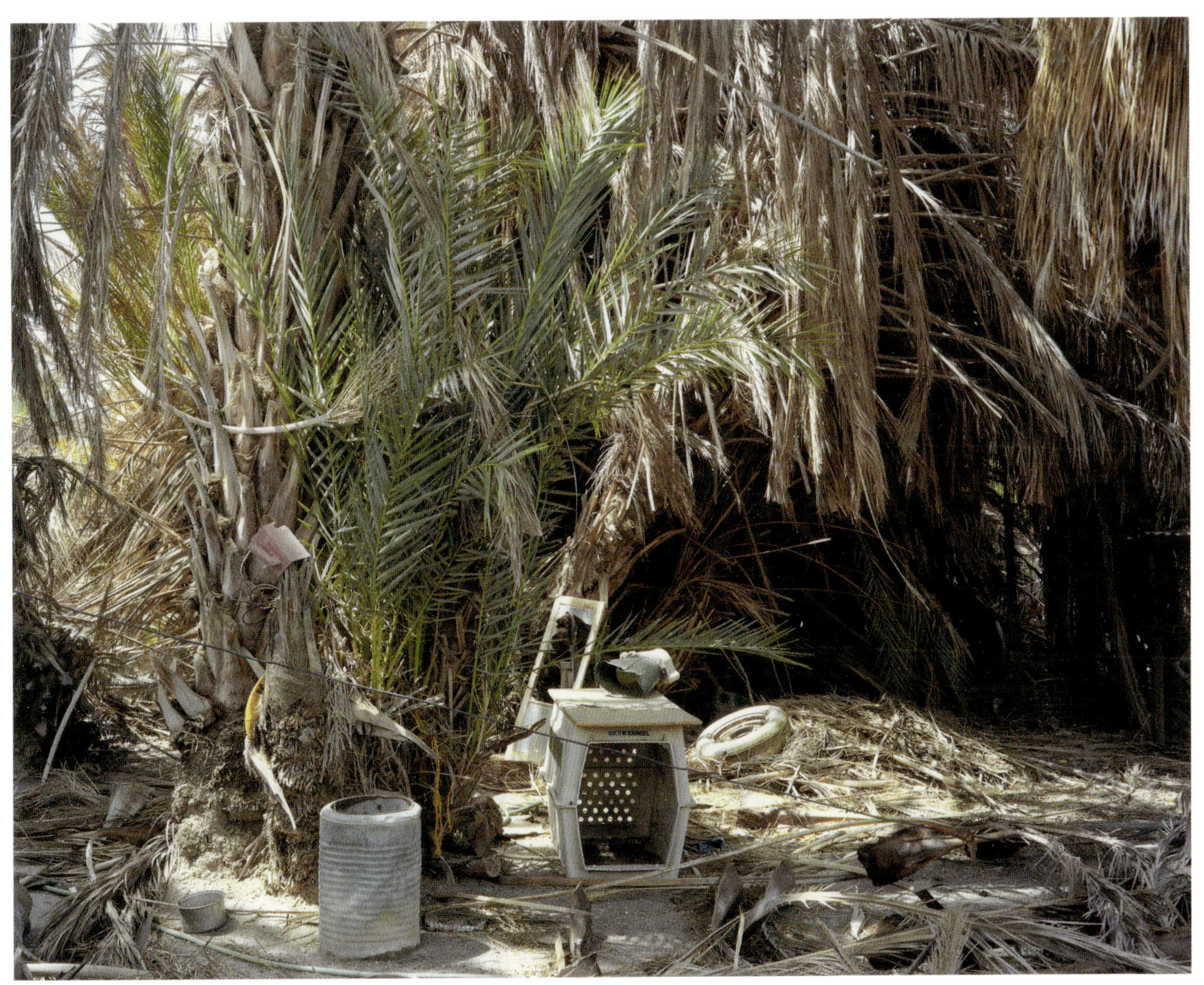

#20 Lucerne Valley, CA, 2007

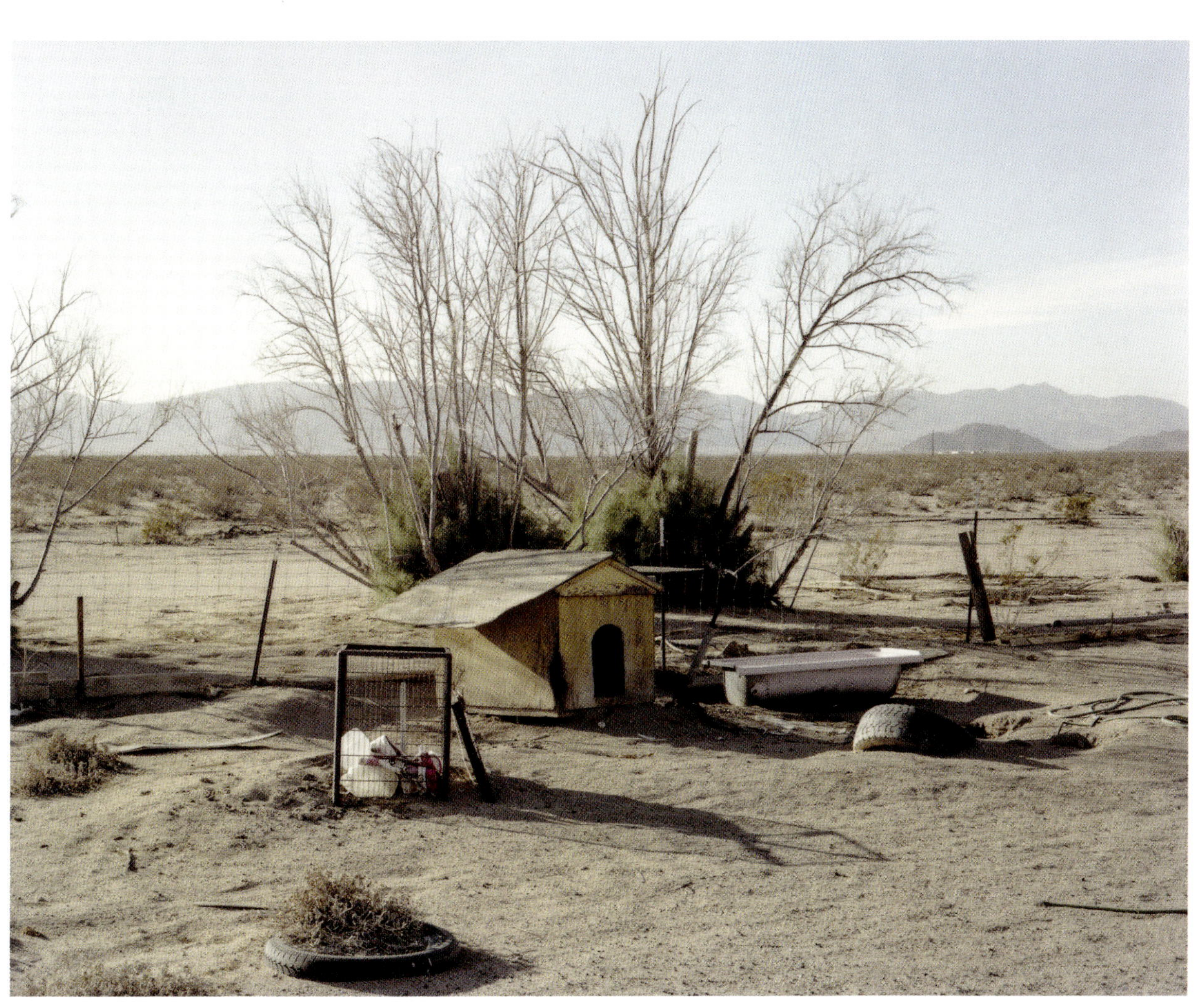

#26A, Antelope Valley, CA, 2008

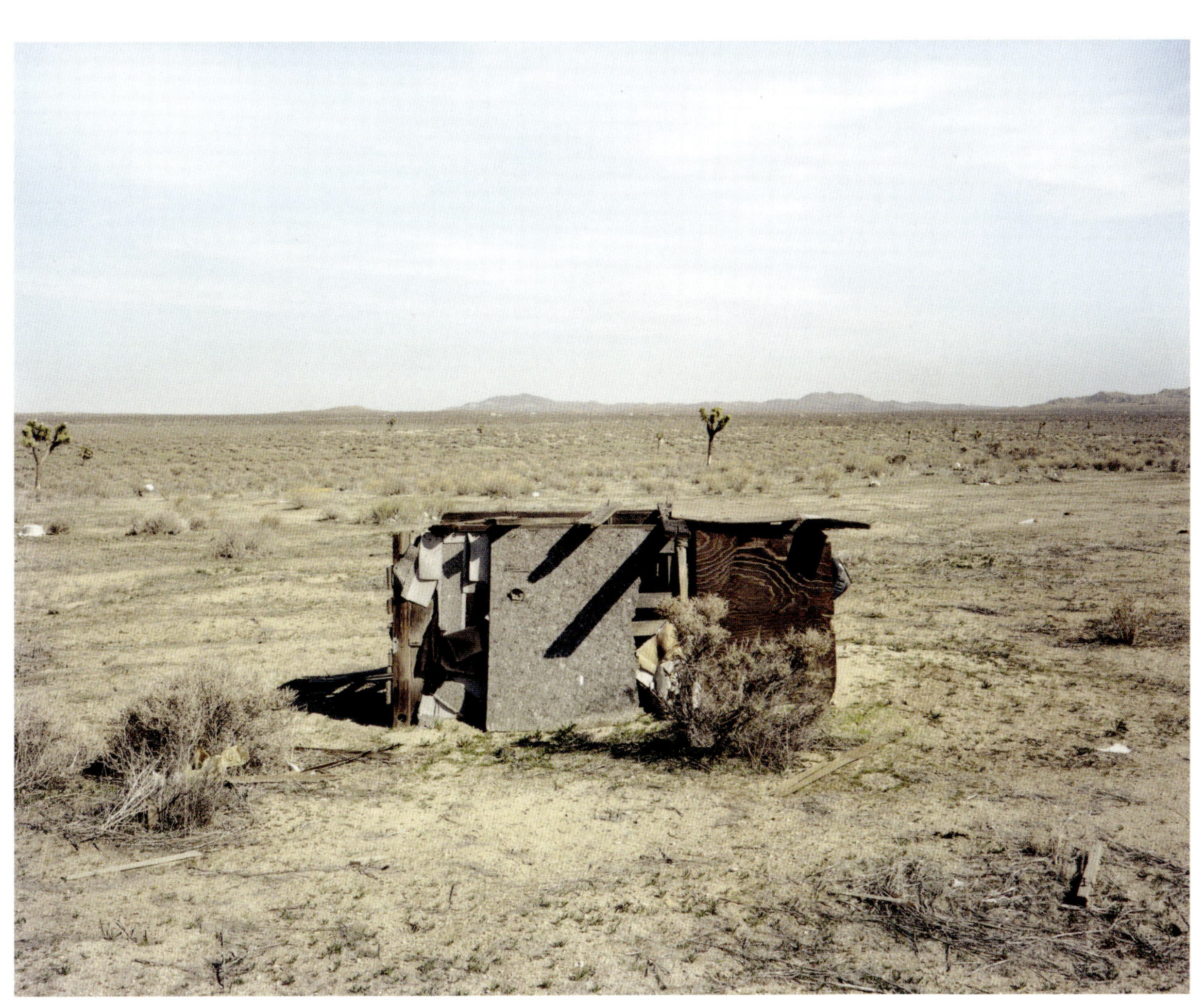

#28 Antelope Valley, CA, 2008

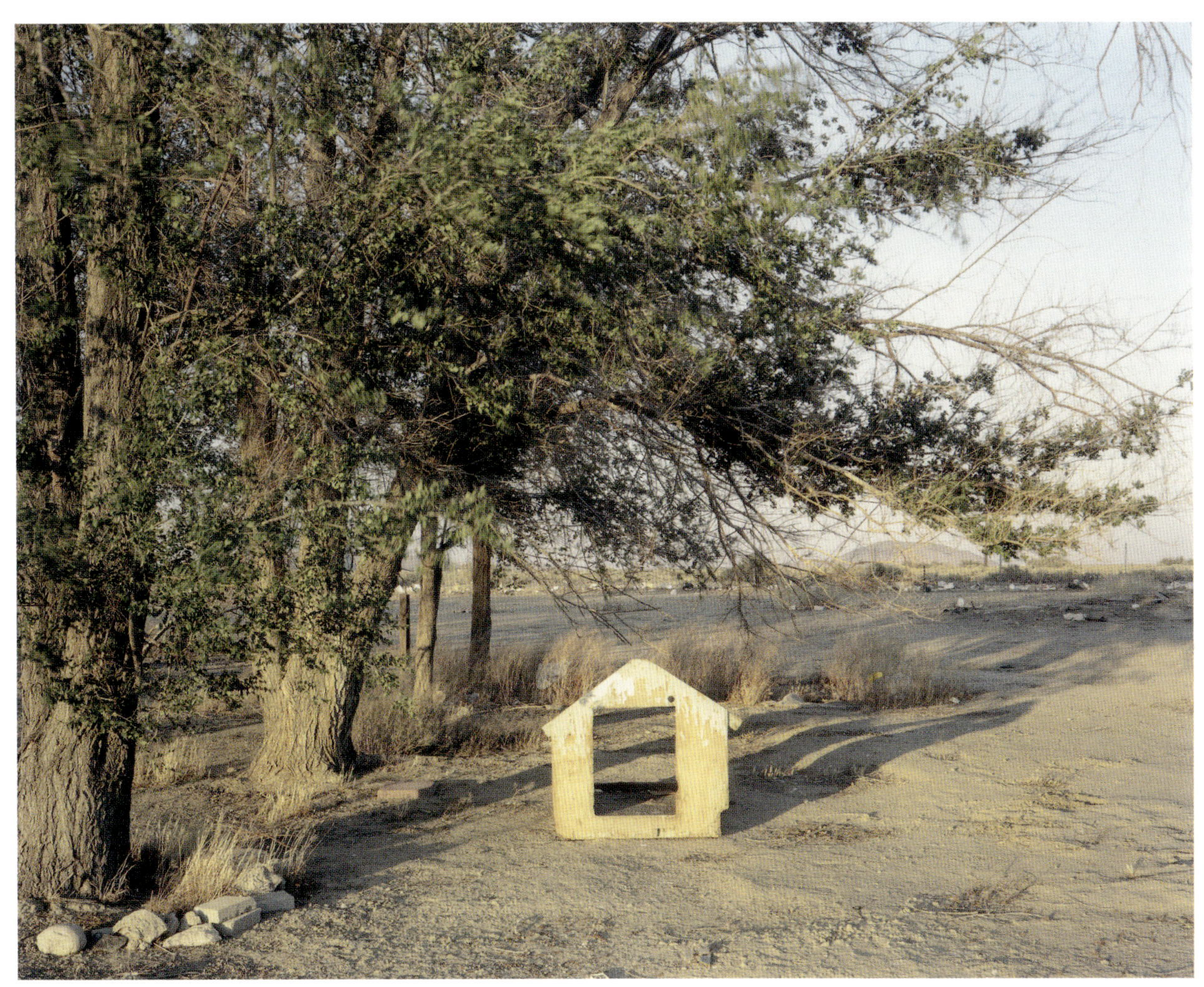

#30 Antelope Valley, CA, 2008

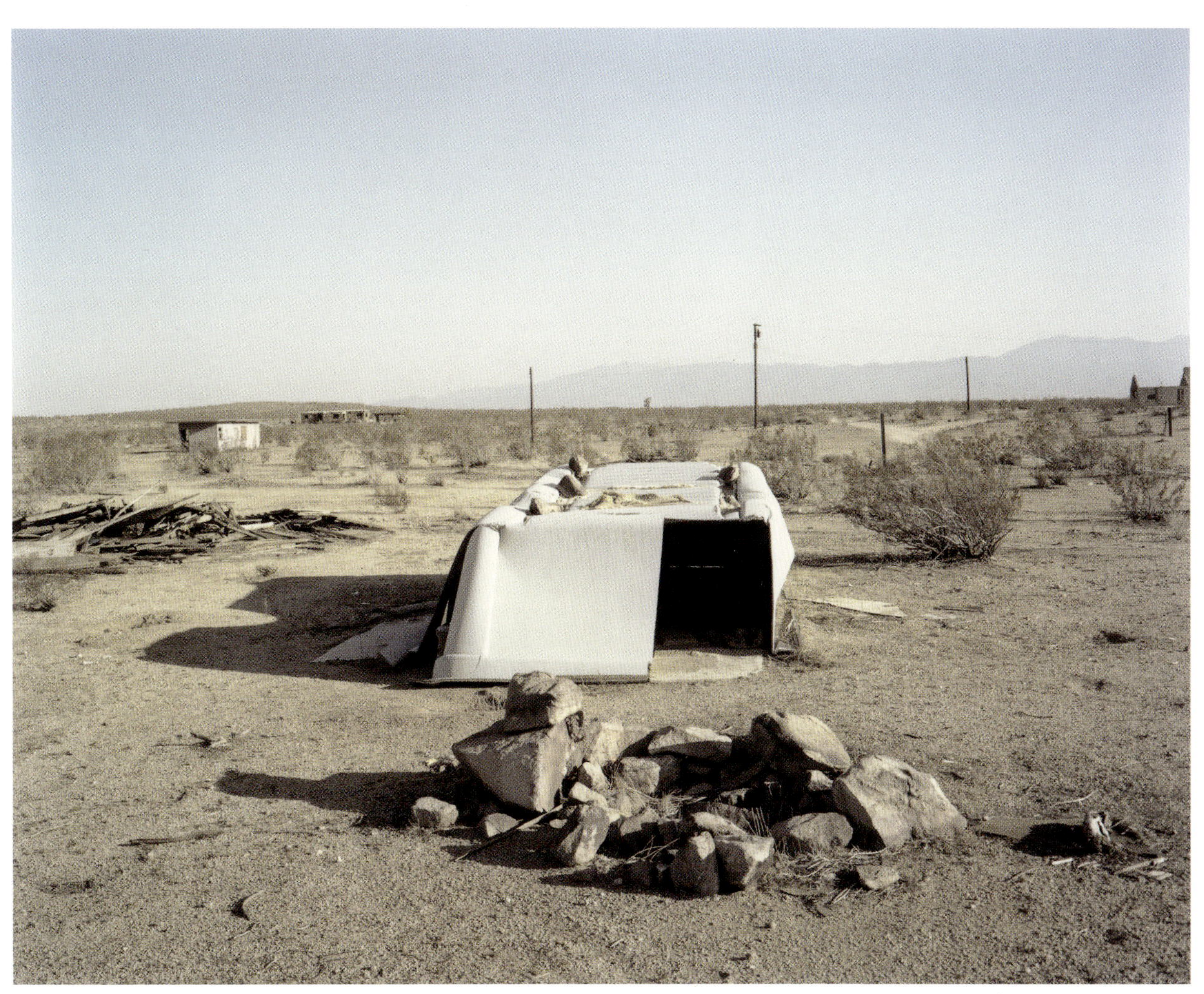

#33 Antelope Valley, CA, 2009

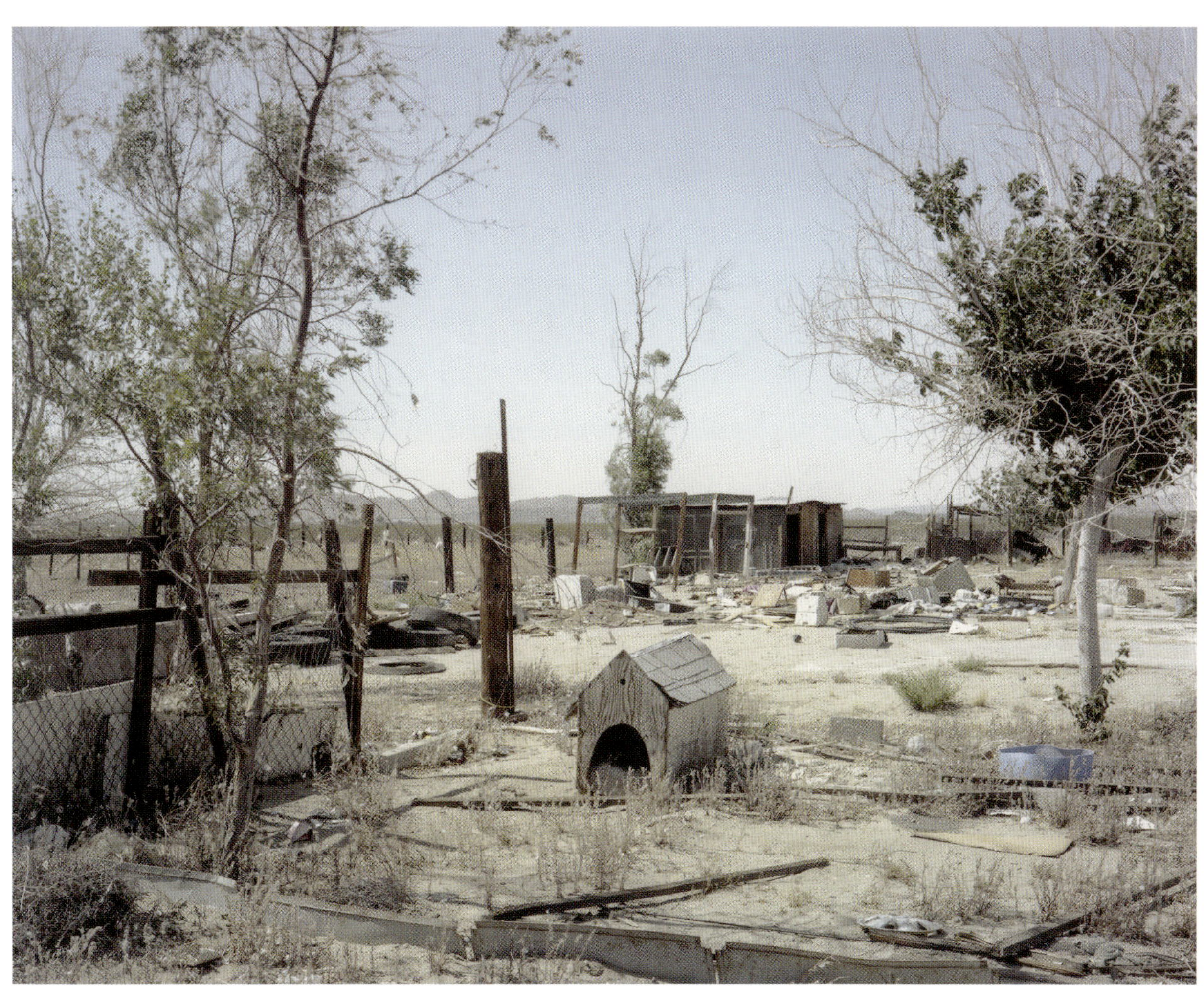

#34 Desert Springs, AZ, 2009

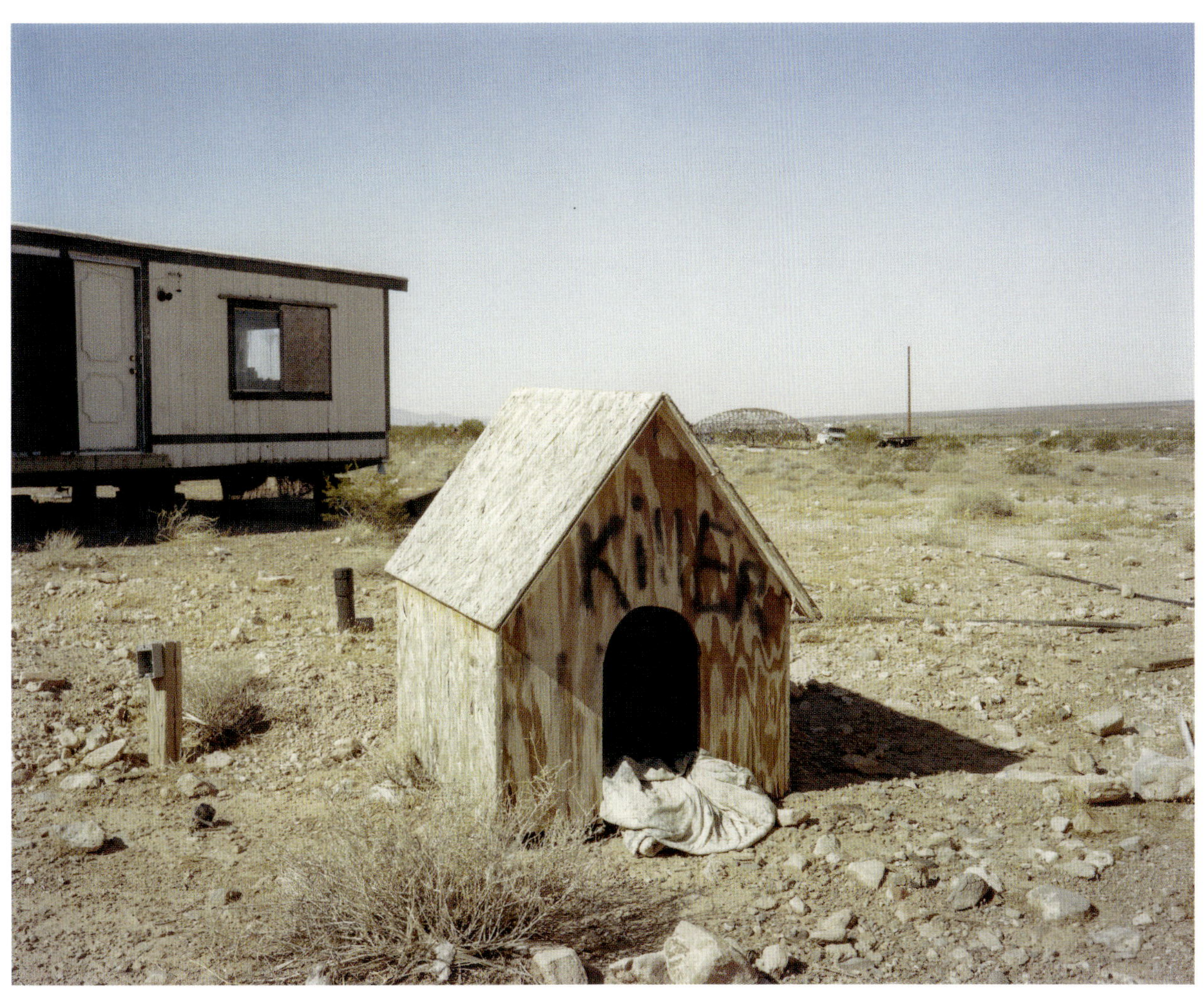
KILLER

#38 Antelope Valley, CA, 2009

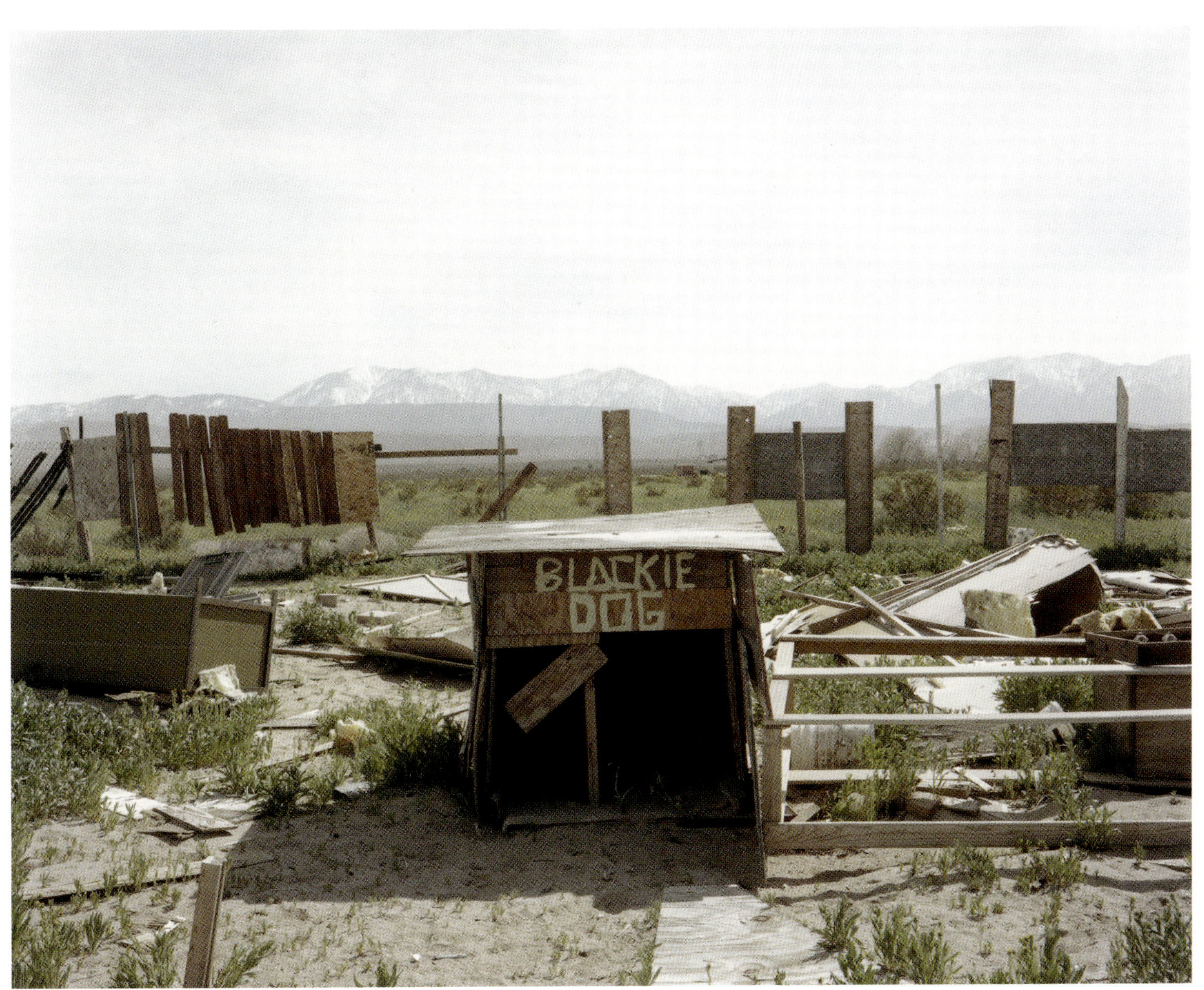
BLACKIE
DOG

#40 Antelope Valley, CA, 2009

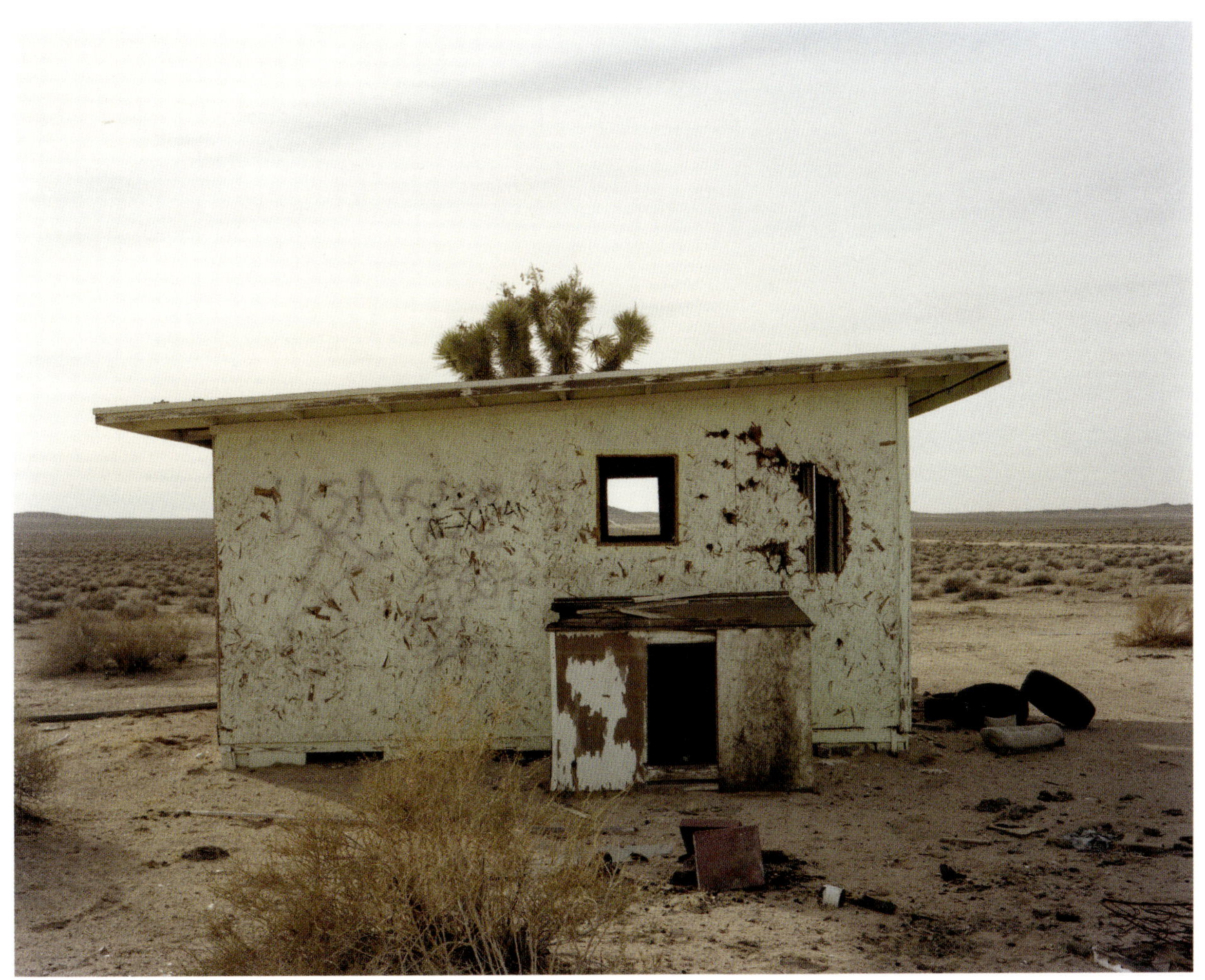

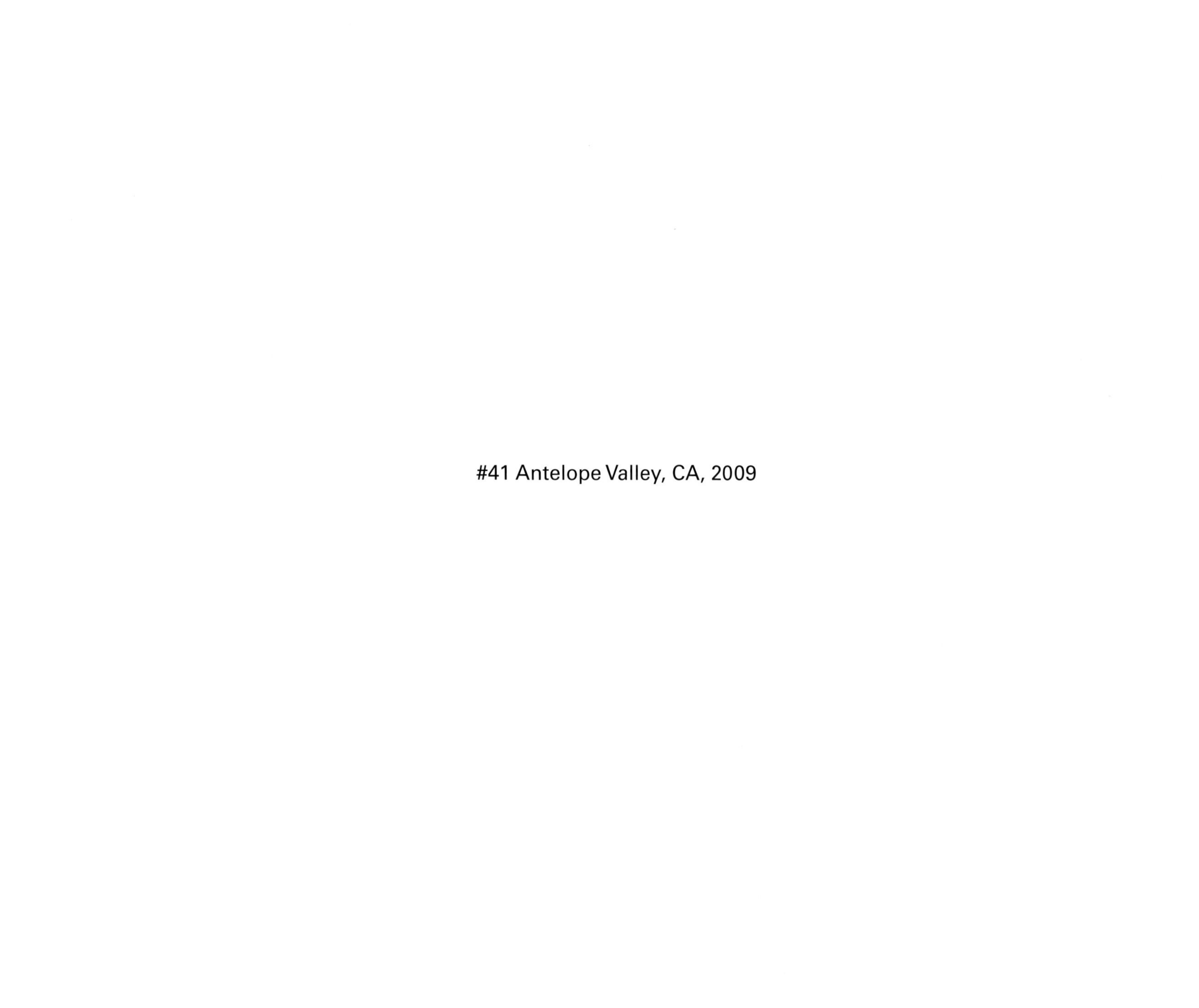

#41 Antelope Valley, CA, 2009

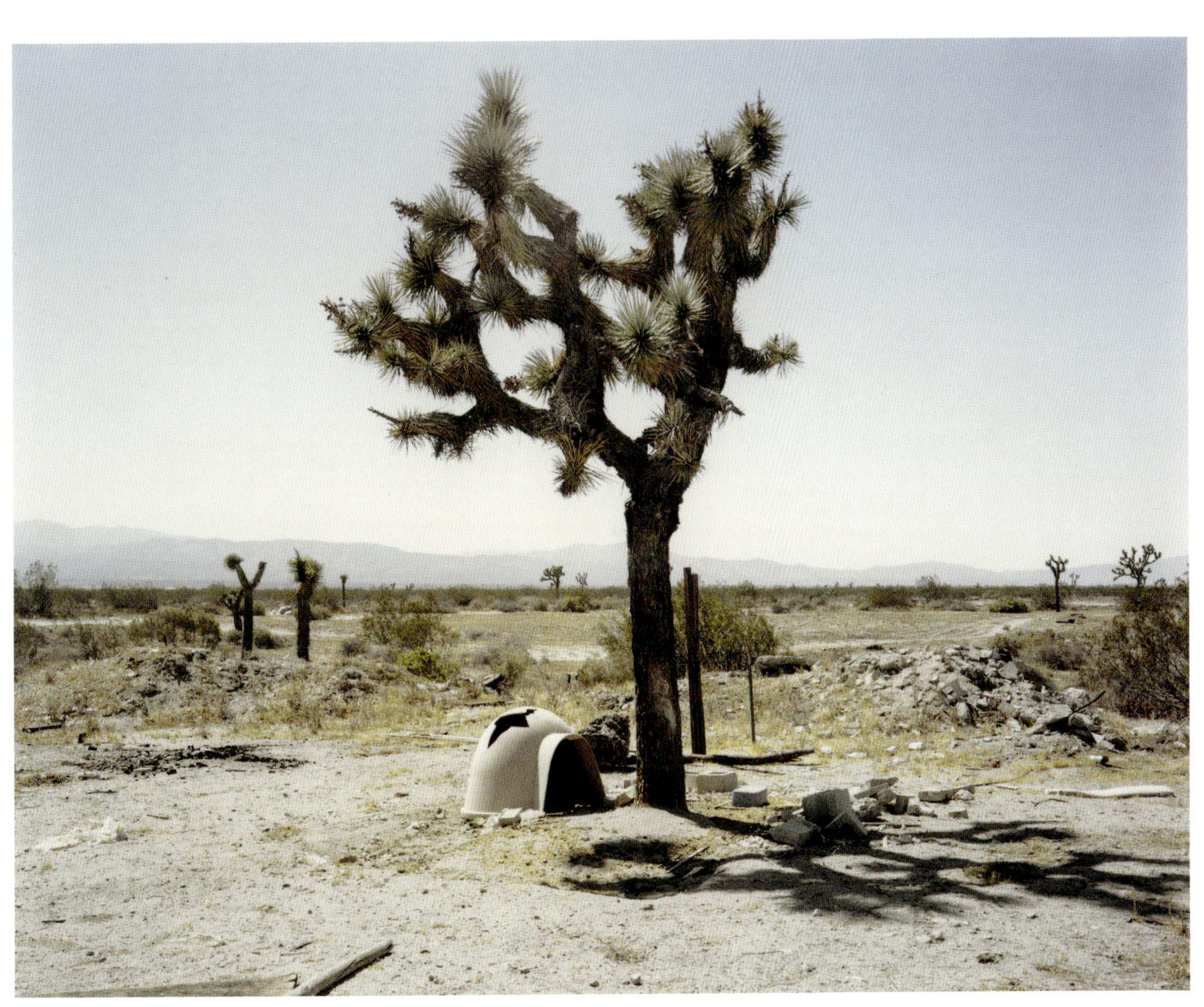

#42 Hinkley, CA, 2010

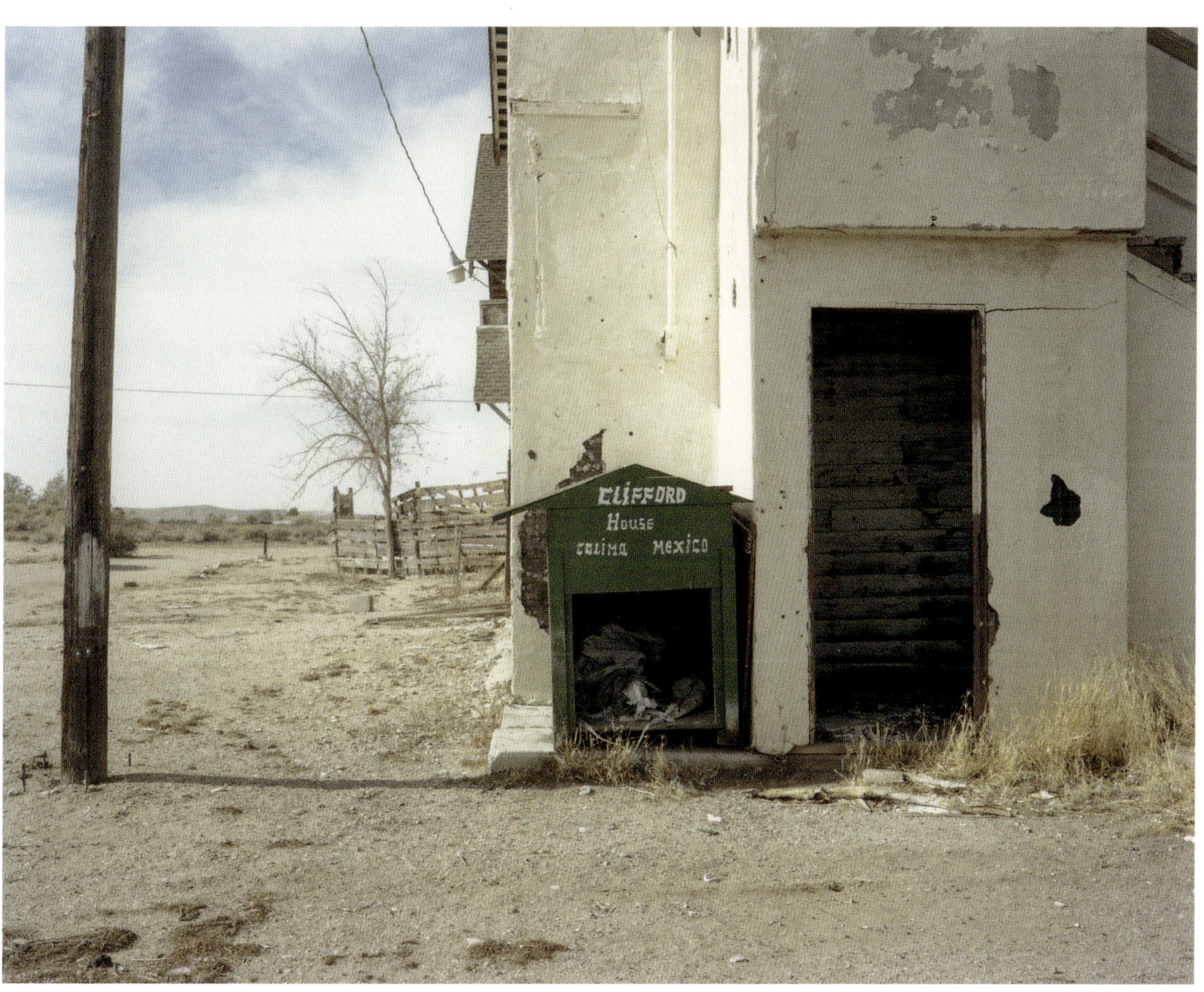
CLIFFORD
House
colima Mexico

#43 Salton City, CA, 2010

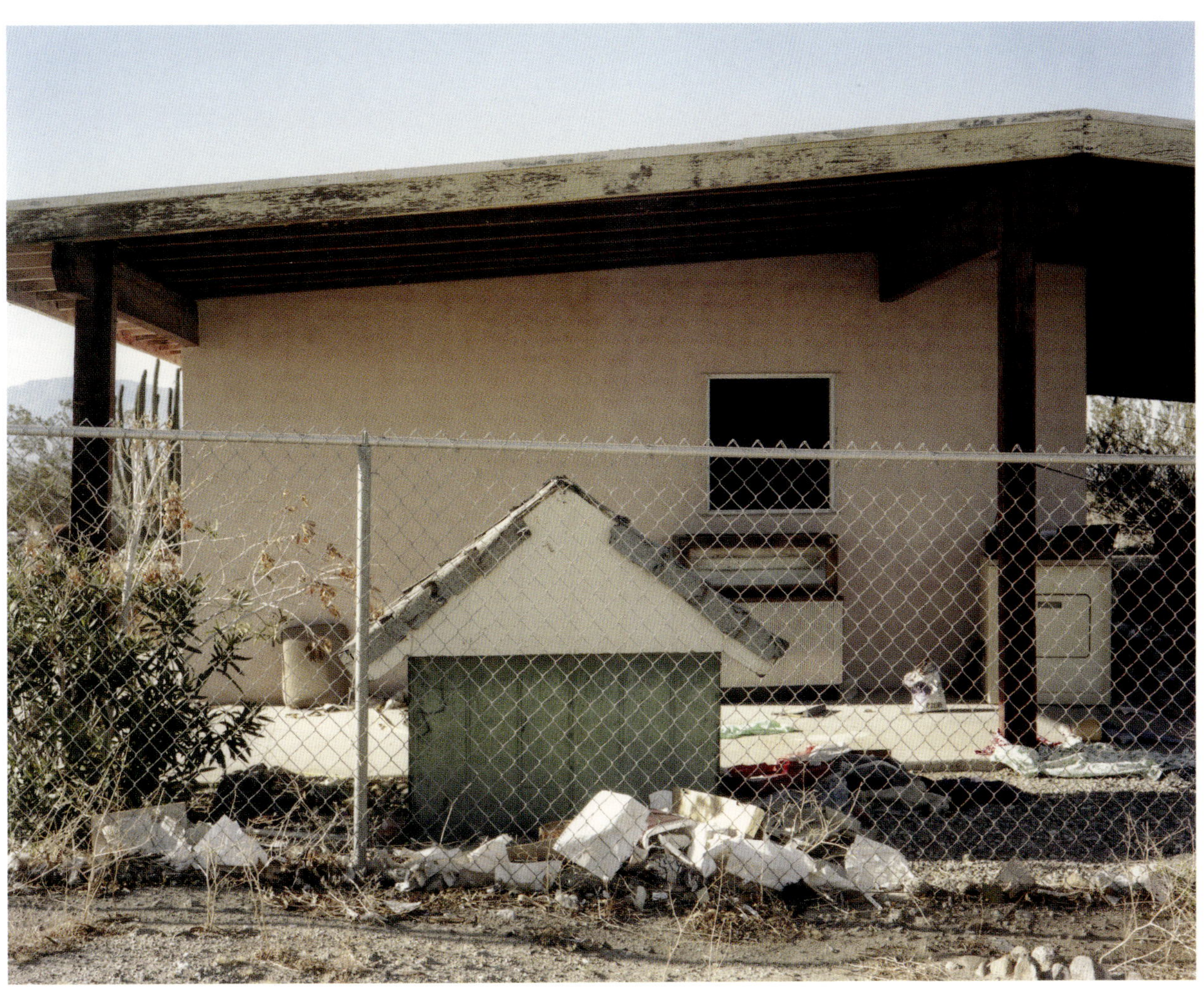

#44 Rosamond, CA, 2010

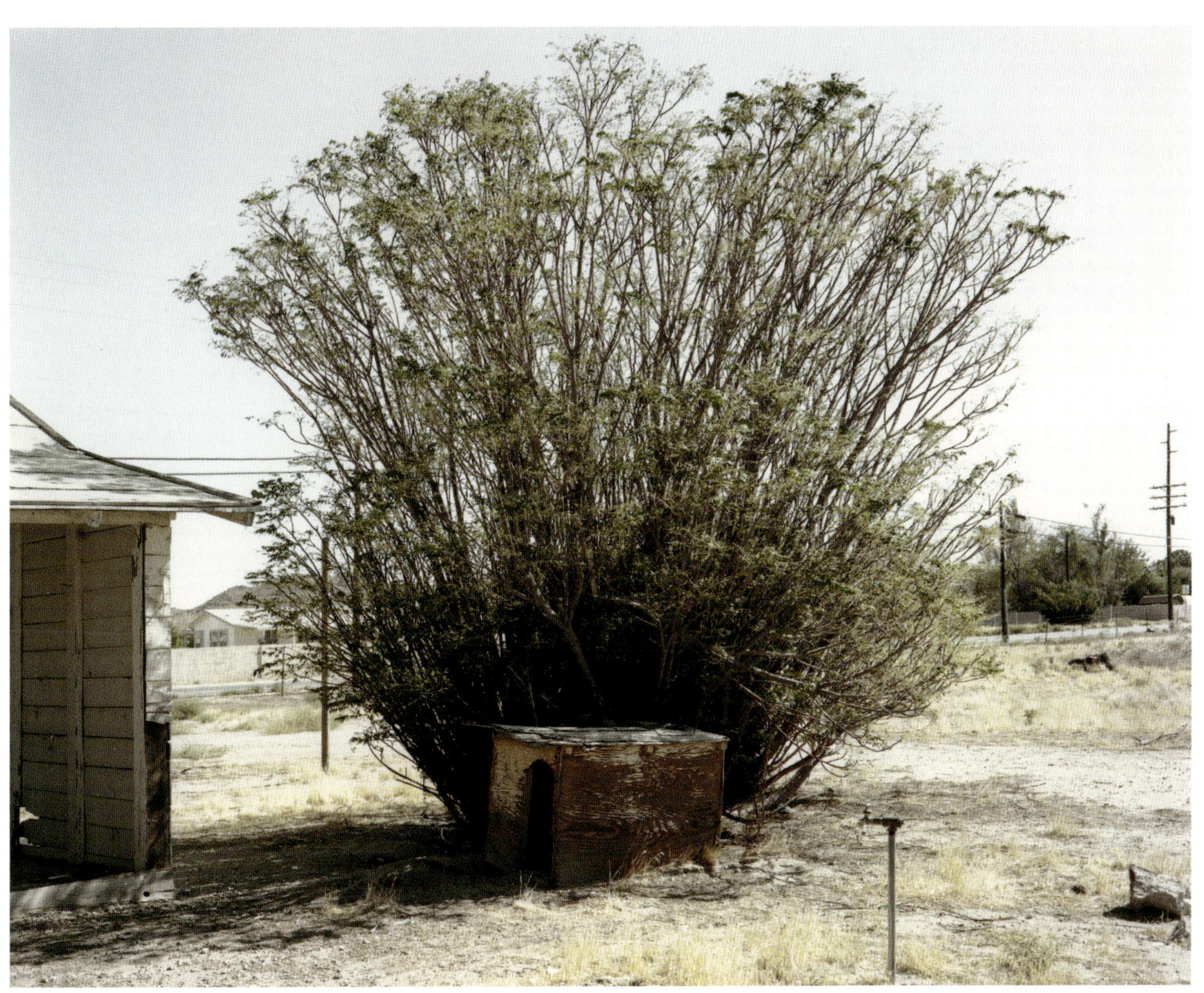

#45 Antelope Valley, CA, 2011

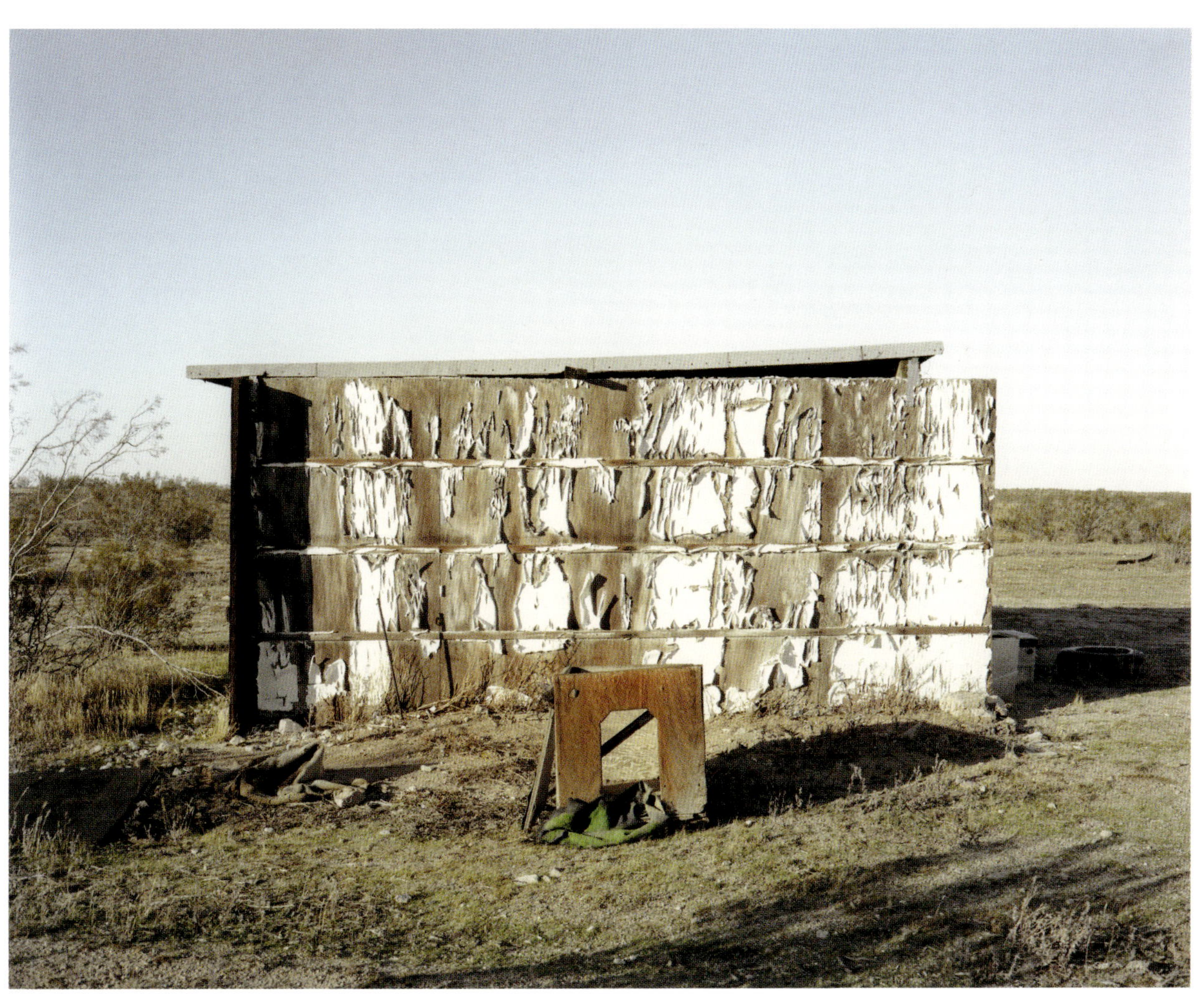

#46 Antelope Valley, CA, 2011

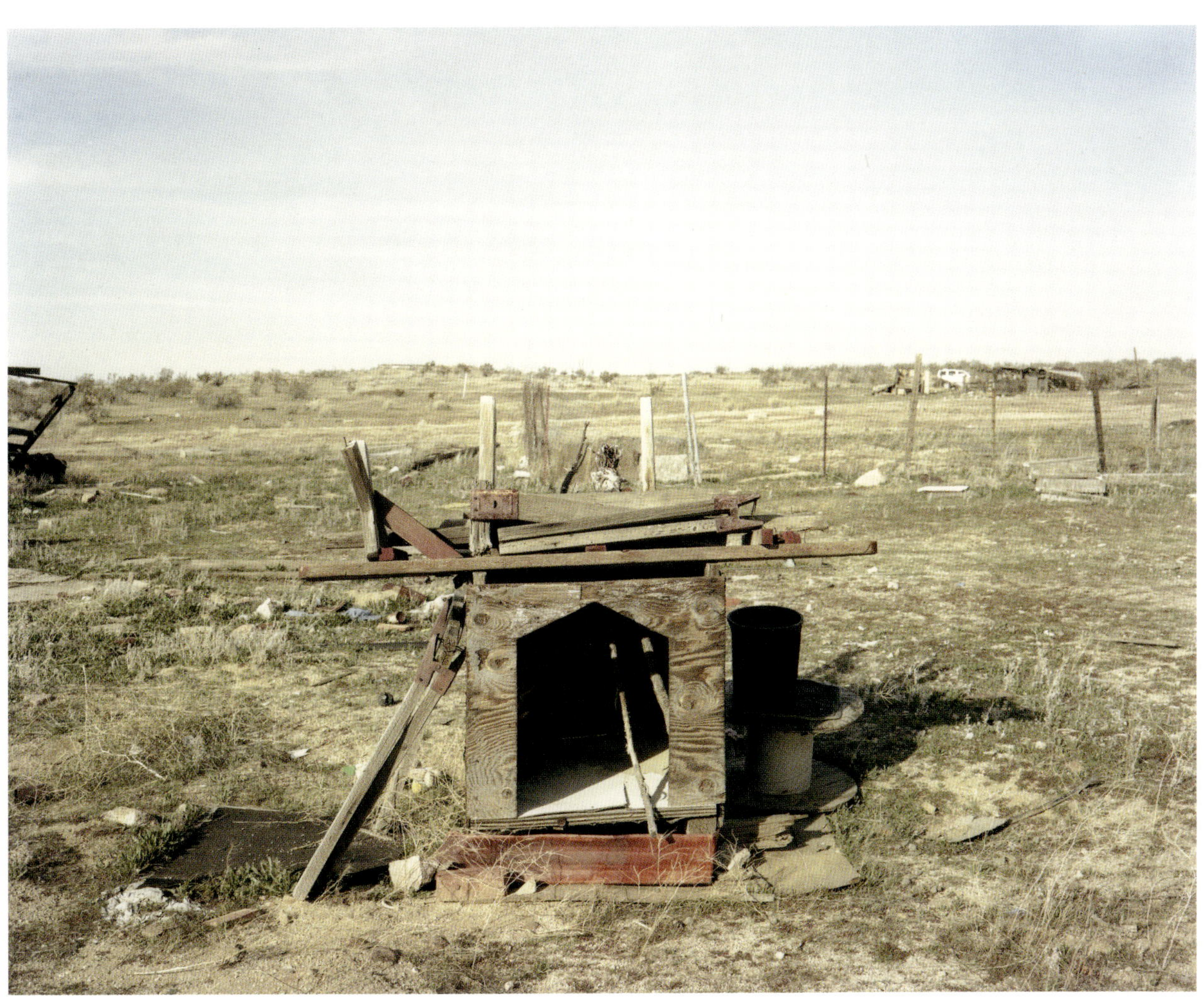

#50 Wonder Valley, CA, 2012

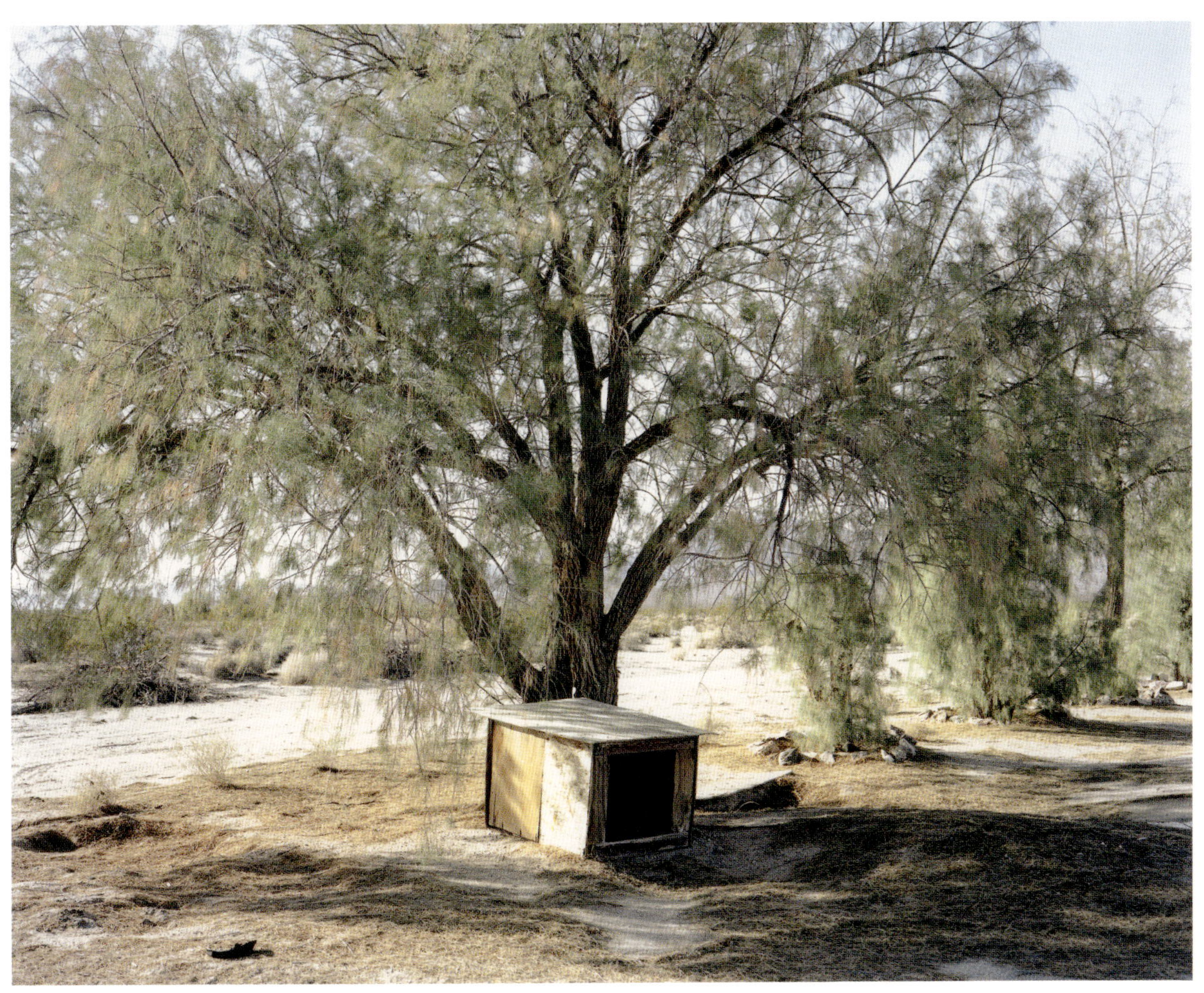

#51 Yermo, CA, 2012

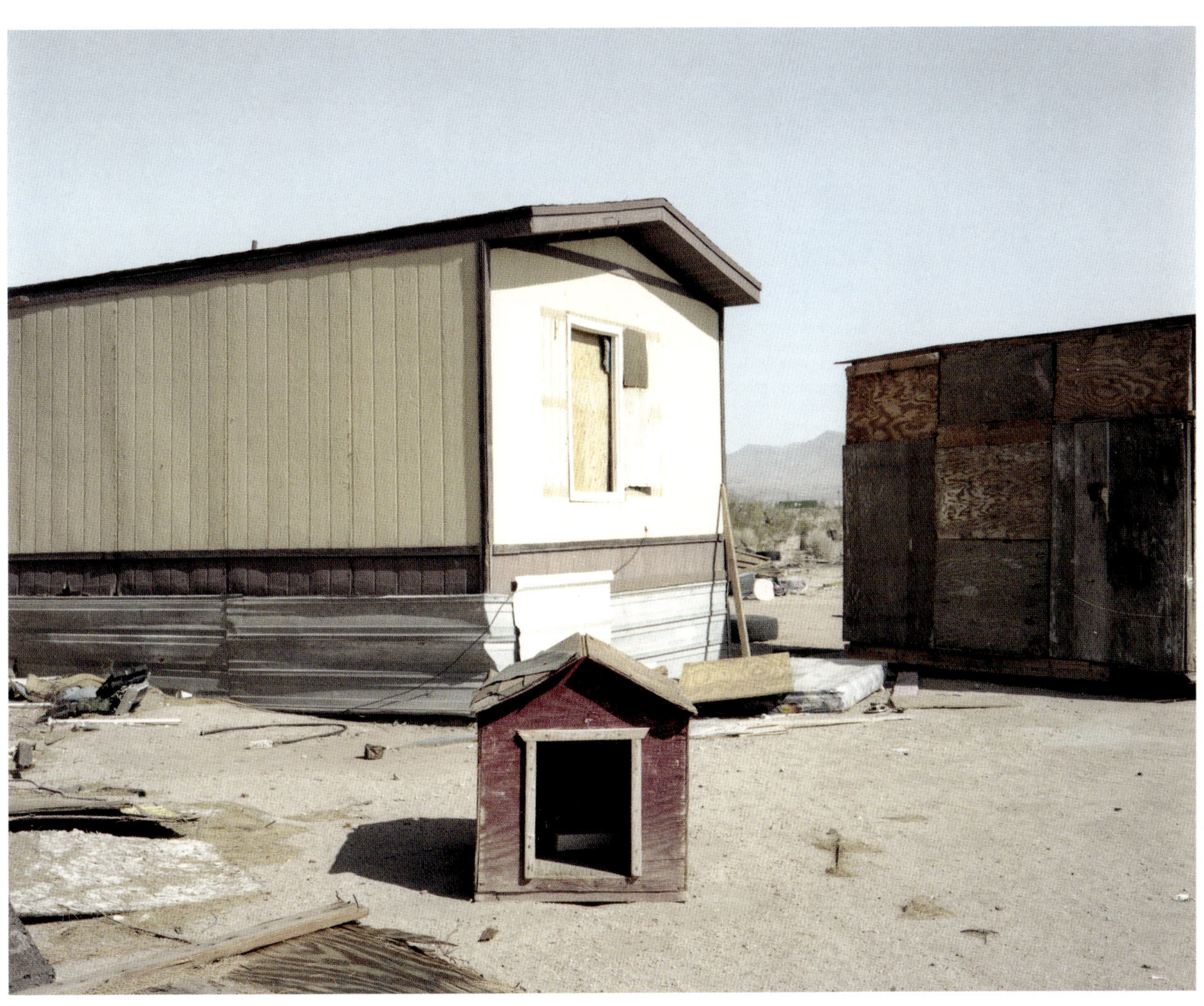

#54 Brisbane Valley, CA, 2013

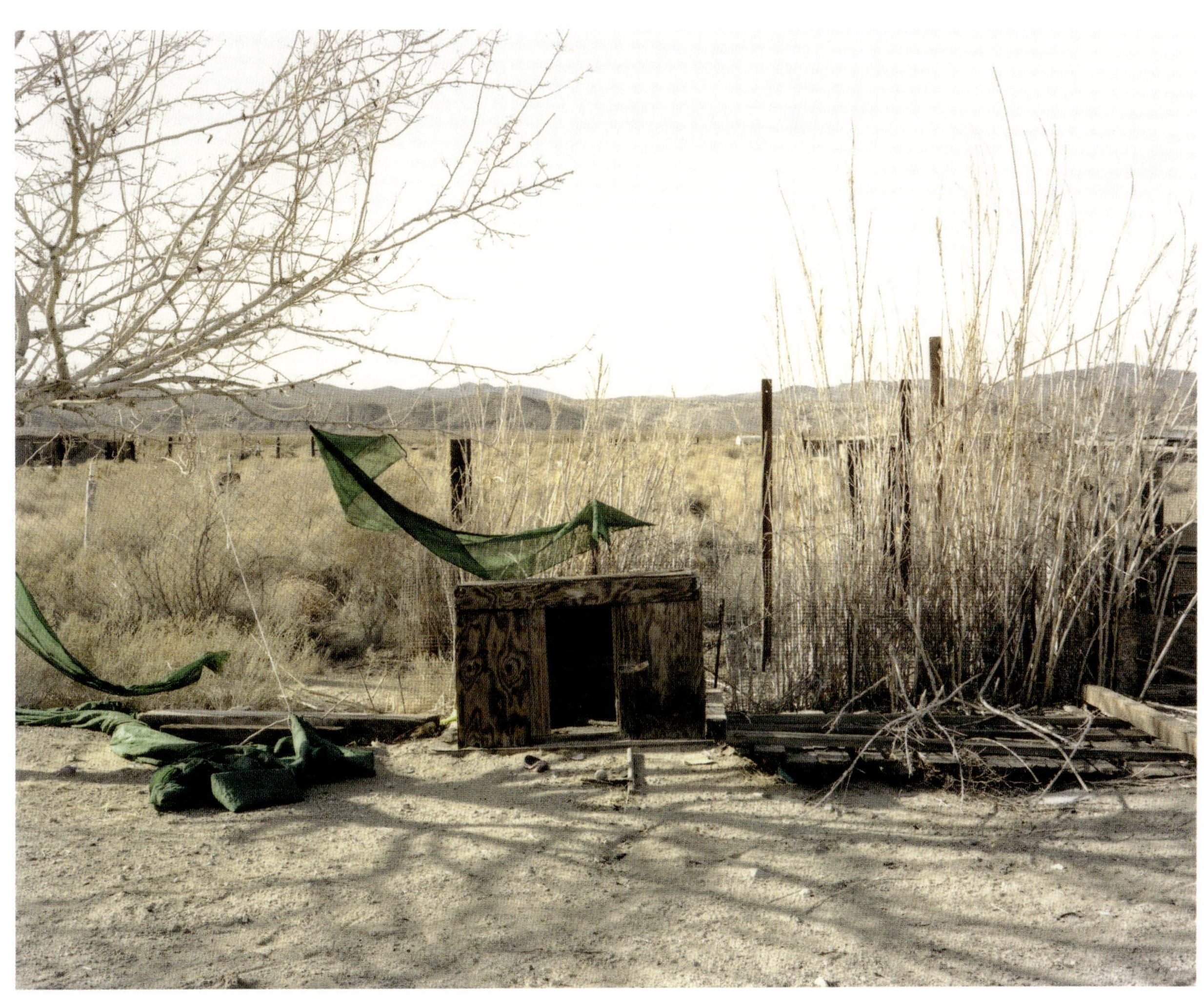

#56 Antelope Valley, CA, 2013

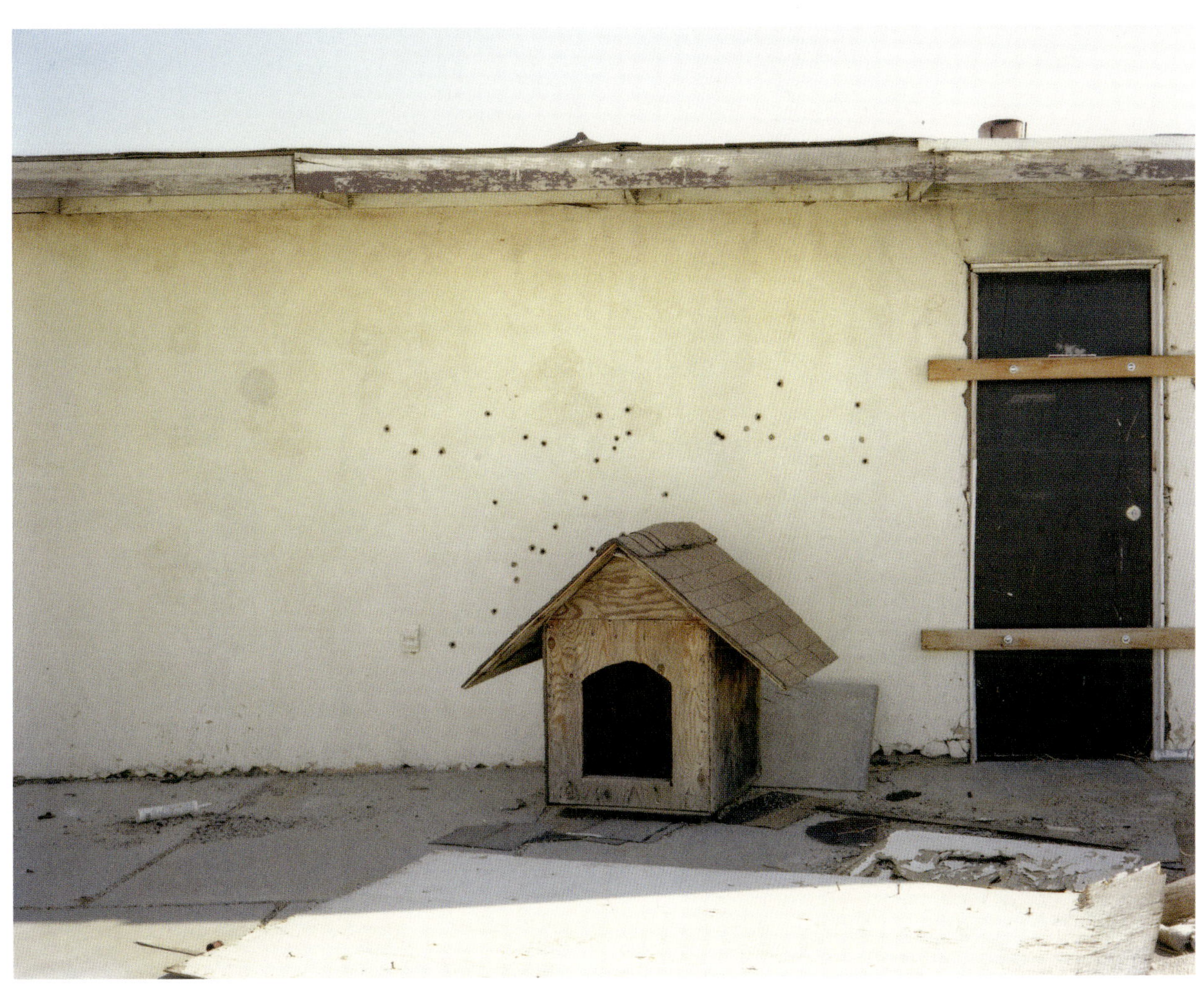

#58 Antelope Valley, CA, 2015

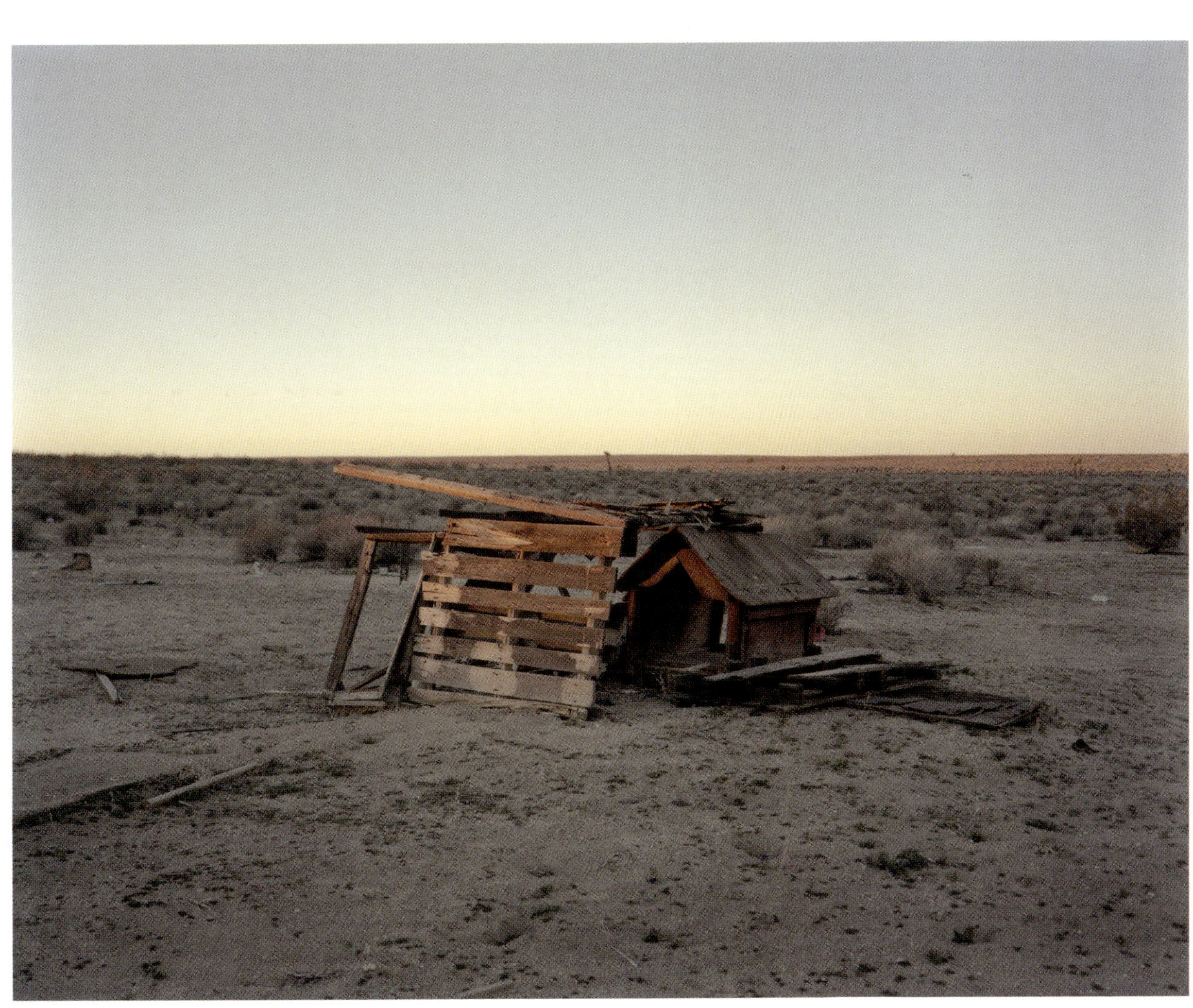

#59 Lucerne Valley, CA, 2015

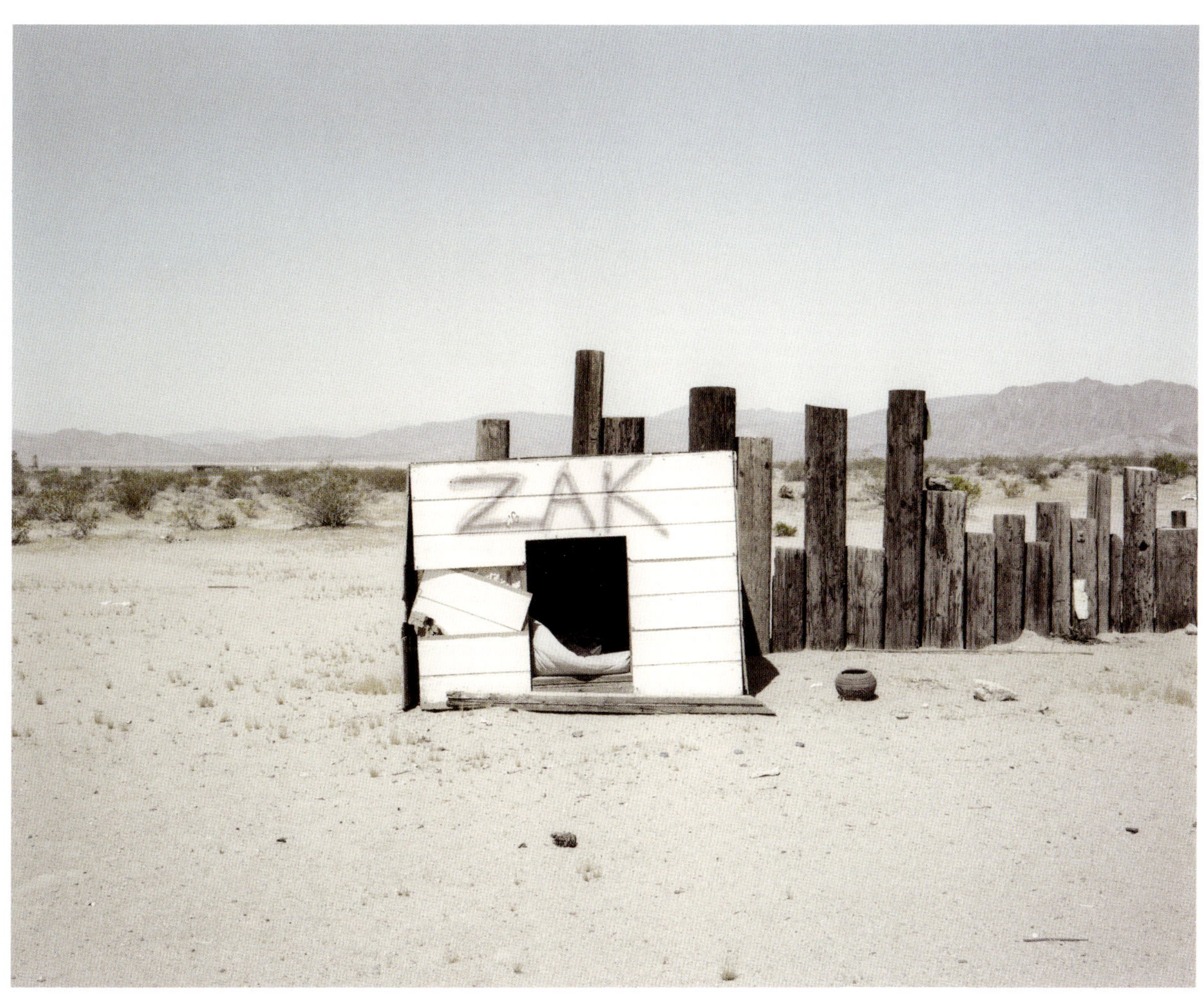
ZAK

In 2003 I had an artist residency at Joshua Tree National Park. I found myself more attracted to the areas outside of the park's boundaries—in particular, Wonder Valley with its hundreds of abandoned houses that I began photographing obsessively. On one of my visits, towards the end of the day, I came upon *Dog House #1* (which actually shows three such houses). I found them to be both sad and funny (I was reminded of the Three Little Pigs). While I had been photographing in black and white, I chose to use color film here. I think it was the light . . .

So, doghouses became something to keep an eye out for. Along with tree houses, bras, vinyl records, etc., they became a collection, a pile to add to when the opportunity presented itself. I never packed up the truck with the idea of going out to photograph abandoned doghouses. The odds were against it. And I wasn't interested in occupied doghouses: that seemed much too complicated, and potentially dangerous.

I drove past *Dog House #2* several times: I really coveted that one but it was not clear if either the doghouse or the people house was abandoned. Finally, I saw someone there. Stopping, I explained my mission but the man did not speak English. In an embarrassing use of my high school Spanish I asked, "Con su permiso," and pantomimed using a camera to photograph the "casa del perro." "Sí." While I set up my 4x5 on its tripod, his entire family gathered behind me at a respectful distance and watched quietly. There was no dog. "Muchas gracias. Buenas días."

That was the only time I spoke to anyone regarding my activity. After that, I never encountered a soul, human or canine, in making these pictures. I still wonder what sort of animal "Killer" was (*Dog House #34*).

Many of these structures conform to a Platonic ideal: the pitched roof and arched opening that signifies "doghouse." Others, however, are more inventive: *Dog House #30* is actually an inverted pickup truck liner with a hole cut into it. Some are merely modified boxes. A few are pre-fabs. And there's the elegant "A" frame of *Dog House #16*. Spencer, my wife's Jack Russell, confirmed several questionable dwellings.

Dog House #59 presented me with a conclusion of sorts: ZAK, the last word in doghouses.

—Mark Ruwedel

For Dunya, Spencer, Betsy, and Eddie—
none of whom lived in doghouses.

I would like to thank Dung Ngo for making this book possible, and Theresa Luisotti for her support of the project, among many other things. And Corrine, who convinced me that having a Jack Russell or two is a good thing.

MR

—

First published in the United States of America by

AUGUST EDITIONS
New York, NY
www.august-editions.com

This first edition is limited to 1,000 copies

© 2017 August Editions
Photos & text © 2017 Mark Ruwedel

Design: Dung Ngo
Color separations: Thomas Palmer

ISBN-13: 978-0-9859958-9-8

All rights reserved. No part of this publication may be reproduced, stored in a retrieval system, or transmitted in any form or by any means, electronic, mechanical, photo-copying, recording, or otherwise, without prior consent of the publisher.

Distributed in the U.S. by RAM Publications + Distribution

Printed in China